BORN FALLING

S.C. SANBORN

Copyright © 2025 by S.C. Sanborn

All rights reserved.

No portion of this book may be reproduced in any form without written permission from the publisher or author, except as permitted by U.S. copyright law.

Contents

1. Cannon Beach — 4
2. Old Souls — 13
3. Through — 17
4. Myrtle Creek — 30
5. Hooky — 45
6. 'Camp' — 49
7. Soul Sister — 68
8. Road Rash — 80
9. Patsy — 87
10. Andy's Van — 95
11. The High Road — 101
12. Craters of The Moon — 113
13. Stag — 121
14. Sunshine — 129
15. Mount Reynolds — 137
16. Mancora — 147
17. Creede — 159

18.	Medford	171
19.	Nowhere, Montana	180
20.	Dunedin	193
21.	Blueberries	197
22.	Yellowstone	201
23.	Somewhere	209
24.	Honeymoon	212
25.	Spiral	216
26.	Don't Go Far	223
27.	Buyer's Remorse	230
28.	Key West	237
29.	DOA	241
30.	Epilogue	248
31.	Acknowledgments	251

Preface

I've never been good at small talk. You know the drill:

"What do you do?"

"Where are you from?"

"Kids? Pets? Hobbies?"

I've spent years dodging those questions. Sometimes I lie. I hate to do it, but it's easier than telling the truth—that my life doesn't belong in polite conversation. Honest answers ruin the mood.

Right now, I'm at a rooftop café in Marrakech. I'm thirty-seven. No kids. No family. My friends are scattered across the world. But I have complete freedom. Terrifying, exhilarating, freedom.

This hasn't always worked out. But it's led me to places I never could have imagined. It's also given me stories worth telling.

Some are painful. Some are funny. Most are both. I have my fair share of lighthearted, anecdotal memories, too. I've woken up naked in enough places to know what a good time looks like. But that was never the point. I'm not sharing my stories to entertain. I'm sharing them to illuminate pain, to give shape to the suffering of my life, and—maybe—to provide a guide for how to avoid the mistakes I made.

These stories are hand-picked and crafted to demonstrate the overarching themes that led to my eventual demise. I've spent a large portion of my life digging into the shadows of my existence. Here, you'll find the truths I found there, dragged out into the open air and hung out to dry.

It was brutal, at times. And yet, there's always a light.

For those readers who find themselves in these pages, know this: you are not alone. This is a map drawn with blood and scar tissue—words from a man who has rarely backed down from a fight. And lost a lot of them in the process.

I've done most of my life on my own. Because of that, I know how it feels to be lost in the dark, and how much it can mean to see someone who has made it through. In the end, what truly matters is reaching back over the ledge once you've made it to the rooftop. This book is my firm, calloused hand, reaching down to help you up. If you need it, take it. If you don't, I am still honored to offer it.

Before we begin, though, it's important to address the limitations of my own perspective.

This is a memoir, the French word for "memory." And memoirs are, like history, written by subjective people. I am no different. My memory is shaped by ego, personality, and the passage of time.

Some of the conversations in this book are amalgamations—synthesized moments filtered through the lens of an often-stunted mind. The beautiful part of being a lifelong writer, however, is that I took notes on pretty much everything, regardless of whatever state of inebriation I might have been in at the time. This, combined with the crystal clarity that a life spent in limbic hijack will give you, has provided a solid baseline to work from.

I also grew up in a constant state of terror. If it wasn't physical danger, it was emotional, psychological, or just good old-fashioned neglect. And as a scared child with intense abandonment issues and a crippling fear of society, I learned to remember the rare conversations I did have. It made me observant—-to an unhealthy degree—to the tenor, timbre, and tone of the people who were speaking to me. I remember things. Especially the words.

All of this also made me self-aware and honest with myself. Brutally so.

Because honesty, despite the occasional trespass, is sacred to me. To lie in these pages would be to lie to the very essence of my being, which believes that we are all one, and to the essence that has kept me alive all of these years. That essence—call it God, spirit, or The Force—is why I am here. It is also quite possible that this is why you're here as well.

So, here we go.

1

CANNON BEACH

I didn't want my book to start with a sad story. No one does.

I wanted to throw these older memories in as flashbacks that surrounded the more entertaining tales I have about my life. But that would dilute the reality, making the hard parts more of a brief interlude, just window dressing along the avenue of joy and highlights. That would be disingenuous.

The beginning of anything is always a reflection of our lives, how it came to be and how we view and process it. These are the parts of my beginnings that I am willing to share. It can't be removed, so it belongs in the front.

Here goes nothing.

***

The beach house was a towering building, built on the side of the hill, near the State Park in Cannon Beach. The paint was new, the lawn was thick grass without weeds, and the hardwood floors were lacquered to a bright shine. Massive windows in the living room held giant, double-panes that looked directly down on the beach below. Usually, he came here alone. He could drink as much as he wanted that way. We all love to feather our gilded cages.

My father had limited custody of my brother and I. We spent one day a week and every other weekend at his house. This gave my mother time to date, party, and drink the way that she wanted. Ostensibly, this was to give us a chance to know our footloose father. For me, it was exciting. My brother didn't see it that way. He avoided the man at all cost. Oddly enough, that wasn't because anything was happening to him. Rather, it was because he had witnessed them happening to me.

I wasn't afraid. I had been conditioned from birth to believe that love came as a byproduct of abuse. Something would happen, then you got hit or screamed at, and then the caregiver would shower you with affection. That was just how it worked. Love and war were one and the same. Fear wasn't part of the calculus. With pudgy legs and soft skin, I would rush headlong into the arms of beasts, unapologetic in my attempts to be loved and recognized. I was a puppy blindly chasing after a ball, despite the insistent barbs coming from the shock collar.

My father used to love playing 'hooky.' It was when he had custody and didn't want to wait for me to be done with school. He would call in, tell them I had another dentist appointment, pick me up, and off we went. My brother usually stayed behind and went home on the bus. This particular Friday was no different.

We stopped for ice cream then roared down Highway 26. We had a dog with us, a small terrier that always smelled horrible. My father hated the poor thing, but I didn't, so it came along. He was my stepmother's and she was a different monster entirely. The runty terrier was just another prisoner of circumstance, biding his time by wagging his tail in a vain attempt to attract the life he deserved.

The polished metal of my father's Cadillac gleamed as if defying the heavy, pregnant clouds above us. The wind whistled from the open window where the dog held his head out of the window.

Both of my parents possessed a Jekyll and Hyde personality. I do not want to imagine what they must have been like together. Luckily for everyone, their marriage ended when I was a year old. When my father was up, he was transcendent, a bright light that lit the darkest recesses of the world around him. This was one of those days. He was the center of attention, the luminous sun drawing people in with compliments, half-hearted promises, and quick jokes. It was all so easy. Life revolved around simple presence in the universe. From ice cream to surfing, we existed solely for the purpose of being free.

Part of the custody agreement stipulated that my father wasn't allowed to drink around us. Even as a young child this had struck me as hypocritical. My mother drank all the time and was horrible when she did. Why was this guy not allowed to do the same? How on Earth was anyone going to show me love and affection if they couldn't get all of the abuse out of the way first? I didn't blame him for ignoring the agreement completely. A Styrofoam cup squeaked and rattled in the cupholder, ice clinking against the straw.

He did make an attempt to hide it from me. He had an obsession with 'supplies,' and would invariably buy way more than anyone could ever need. Then later, underneath the mountains of fruits and vegetables crammed into the fridge, there was always a large case of Budweiser. Maybe two. I never looked too deeply into it. I would grab my orange and carefully rearrange everything so he wouldn't know I had discovered his treasure.

As soon as we got into town, we went to the local market. He took his time chatting up the women behind the counter. After he finished, the bags were piled so thickly on the backseat that the dog was having a hard time navigating it all. As soon as the car stopped rolling, he begged to be let out. Soon, the tufts of his gray fur were lost in the rolling dunes of the nearby beach.

Inside there were three separate floors that could house an entire family. My room was in the basement. This made sense to me, even then. The basement is where you store the things you want to keep quiet and out of the way. I ran downstairs and checked on my Teenage Mutant Ninja Turtles blanket. I brought it with me everywhere I went. At least, I thought I did. Really, it was just the same blanket in five different locations. Some people like towels, but personally, I've always been a solid proponent of good blankets. They keep you safe from monsters.

The central heating kicked on with a heavy thrum as the wind picked up. The large bay windows stood soundless and immobile, but the kites and windchimes outside showed the flurry of cold air coming off the water. The dog appeared, soaked and panting, his tongue lolling to the side. He came inside and immediately started shaking, drawing the ire of my father. I quickly ran to the bathroom, grabbed a hand towel, and began to dry the soaked fur. As I frantically wiped dirty water from the floor, I looked up to see my father glowering. Then he receded into the kitchen.

I sat at the large dining room table. Judging by the rapidly fading light outside, it was sometime around dusk. He had cooked something for dinner. I loved it when he cooked, because I got to drink soda. Lots of it. Regardless of whether I had finished the one in my hand, he would crack another and bring it to me. I couldn't have possibly guessed that he was cracking two at the same time.

I lost track of all of the times I'd been hit and tossed around. The summer before, my stepmother had planned a family vacation. They had rented a farmhouse in the countryside somewhere. I had done something wrong and she had screamed at me to get inside and 'wait for my father.' I knew what that meant. I sprinted to my room in the basement, bolted the door, and hid in the closet. I fucked up though— I forgot my blanket on the bed.

It had only taken him a few minutes of kicking and ramming before he had knocked the door off of its hinges, found my hiding place, and pulled me out by my hair. As my vision swam, I grabbed the leg of the rickety bed, feeling the leg coming loose from the rest of the frame. He pulled again and it came free. Punches rained down. Somehow the leg thrust upward at the right time and in the right place, stunning and knocking him into the wall.

I had the strange impulse to continue, relentlessly attacking... Instead, I threw the long piece of wood down to the floor and ran out of the house. There was a field there, stretching out toward the horizon. Years had passed since someone had mowed it. I crept down into one of the hedgerows and dug myself into the warm, stony ground. No one came looking for me.

Later that night, we all sat down to dinner. My stepmother asked questions and dictated the conversation. It was as if nothing had happened. My brother and stepsiblings kept their eyes glued to the table. None of them really looked at me anymore.

The memory of that trip stirred in my mind as I sat there and stared at the wood-paneled ceiling, the massive windows, the art work on the walls. As I did, I felt the energy shift as keenly as a bird riding a thermal. When either of my parents shifted from one polarity to the other, I could feel it deep within my bones. It's a survival instinct. I could hear him laughing to himself and muttering about women. Never a good sign. Women hadn't been good to that man and vice versa. I knew then that it was only a matter of time. Like a moth to the flame, however, I walked around the corner. He was sitting on a chair in the kitchen, his back to me. I reached my hands around his neck and gave him a big hug.

"I love you, Dad. I'm gonna go watch a movie."

He said nothing and put a cold hand on top of mine. I breathed a huge sigh of relief that I didn't fully understand as I reached the bottom of the stairs. There was an enormous couch in the basement, L-shaped, with removable cushions. It was perfect for making forts. I put my favorite Star Wars movie on and pulled my blanket tight to my neck.

Soon enough, I got hungry. That's what happens when you give a kid a bunch of sugar. They eventually crash and need more. I couldn't hear anything from upstairs, so I figured that my father had migrated to his room on the top floor. A vague feeling of terror crept under my skin as I reached the top of the stairs. I took a big breath and thought about what one of my teachers had said: that the only way to beat the monsters in the closet is to face them head on. I stood up straight and balled my fists, then ran down the hall toward the fridge...

When I reached the kitchen, I pulled open the door, grabbed a can of orange soda, and... dropped it onto the floor. The racket was amazingly loud as the can detonated on the ground, spraying in all directions. Everything froze. My heart, my mind, and time itself. Terror raced up my spine in a frozen rope. I immediately heard his voice from behind me.

"GodDAMNit BOY."

He was sitting in the same place I'd left him. He wasn't a large guy. Maybe 5 foot 6 on a good day. He blended in well into the dark scenery of the kitchen. Maybe he had fallen asleep and slumped into his chair. Regardless, he was behind me, angry, and I had made a mess. Not good. I ran to the sink and grabbed a hand towel.

"It's okay... it's okay... I'll just..."

But he already had me by the shoulder. I slid through the slick soda pop... He was dragging me to the basement. I kicked out and tried to grab hold of the railing, but I was already sailing through the air. I landed face first on the bottom of the landing, about twenty steps below.

Luckily, none of my bones broke. I crumpled to the first landing, sliding across the soft wood to the elaborately paneled wall. I knew better than to stay down. When a monster's blood is up, it is best to run. Fast. Terror surged through my veins, fueling me past the pain. I got up, limping heavily, and jumped down the second set of stairs. At the bottom was a narrow hallway. I bounced off the wall and fled on trembling legs. Thunderous steps echoed down the stairway behind. I could see my shadow in front of me.

Down the short hall, I sprinted into the den, past the massive couch. My room was at the end. The scene where Luke and Leia are chasing the stormtroopers on hoverbikes was on the TV. I ran like a hunted animal, wildly flailing into my room. I slammed the door, turning the lock just as his body weight hit the outside. I raced to my backpack.

Where I grew up, you either learn quickly or you die. I'd known this for a long time. These assholes didn't remember what they did the next day. And they were expert liars when they could be bothered to try. I ripped out the massive door stopper I had stolen from my school, lunged forward, and jammed it underneath the doorframe.

I assumed that if I was quiet, then I could hide. I closed the closet door silently, spinning the knob softly so that the latch slowly moved past the strike plate. I wasn't worried anymore. This time, I had remembered to grab my blanket. I pulled the thick fabric up over my head and huddled, crouched against the sloped wall behind. He tried to get in for a while. I was a cornered fawn, too tired to run any further, hoping that the lion would just get tired enough to fuck off. He gave it one last shove, then shuffled back upstairs. The noise quickly subsided.

I woke up still in the closet. A splitting headache seared into the right side of my skull. My joints ached, and sharp pains came from my left side. I couldn't see any bruises but I knew they would appear soon. A scratching sound came from the hallway. The dog was outside my door, whining to be let out. I took out the door stopper and furtively poked my head out. Silence. With shaking hands, I scooped up the poor little beast and darted outside. The sound of the surf pounding carried away the lingering fear. It was a short walk to the beach. When we hit the sand, we kept walking.

It took a while for them to find me. First, it was the sheriff. I guess a kid walking by himself with no shoes, a small dog, and a multicolored blanket across his shoulders was easy to spot. The man yelled gruffly, telling me to stop and wait where I was. Then my father showed up. For some reason, I was ushered me into my father's car. I still wonder what he told them.

The drive home was a mixture of rain pouring down the window, plaintive cries from the backseat, and Jerry Jeff Walker playing quietly in the background. After a while we stopped at a diner for breakfast. We had been there before. They had amazing pie. They handed me a kid's breakfast menu, but I ordered a slice anyway. My father didn't bat an eye as the waitress looked at him. When she walked away, he looked right at me. I remember his exhausted, bloodshot eyes. His faraway stare. The gaunt look of his cheeks and the smudge on the bottom of his glasses.

"I'm sorry," he said.

I didn't respond. I just ate my pie and smiled. This was the good part, the point where the bad stuff had already happened. Now I would get whatever I wanted for the rest of the day. For some reason though, all I remember wanting was to get back 'home,' whichever house that was that particular day. I missed my Star Wars action figures.

The rest of the ride was smooth and uneventful. I stared out the side window, the rain casting deep streams backwards across the pane. After a while, I closed my eyes and pretended to sleep.

2

OLD SOULS

The door closed behind me with a familiar click. I could hear the principal shuffling papers behind it. The visits didn't faze me anymore. Every day was another bully, another fight. My brother was one year older. His friends took turns trying to pick on me. They were mean.

I was meaner.

I'd gotten detention again. It was a gift. The student-teacher who watched over it always read to me and I usually got a ride home from one of the other kid's parents. As I passed through the office, I waved to the receptionist, an elderly woman with bee-hive hair that seemed alive in the bright fluorescent lighting. She smiled at me as I passed, then reached out and grabbed me by the arm. With her other hand she licked her thumb and wiped the remnants of lunch from my cheek. I grinned and skipped through the front door.

Playful screams echoed across the concrete playground. Teachers were posted here and there, all of them absent-mindedly watching over the chaos. One of them turned as I walked nearby. He was the school counselor, the only one who had ever asked about the bruises on my arms and legs. He never did anything about it. No one did. I knew that no one could keep me safe, anyway. Adults were best avoided. I kept my eyes forward and started running toward the field. My friends were there, playing soccer in the grass.

I knew things back then—things a nine-year-old kid has no business knowing. I knew how to mask and protect myself, how to fight, how to lie, and most importantly, how to survive. I also knew, from the bottom of my heart, that life is pain. I know now that we're not here to curse the rain, but rather to learn to dance in it—happily, and without the influence of drugs, sex, or alcohol to grease the gears. To a lesser extent, I knew that even then. And that's not a good thing for a child to know. That might be why the other kids would often approach me, oftentimes out of the blue, to talk about what was going on in their lives.

Her name was Erin. She had sat next to me in kindergarten, always willing to let me use her crayons and puff paint when I 'forgot' mine at home. She walked straight through the soccer game and started tugging on my shirt sleeve. Tears streamed down her face. She stammered out some sentences in quick succession, asking if we could talk. It was about her parents. They were getting divorced.

The question didn't faze me in the least. There was no telling how she knew my parents were separated. Maybe it was common knowledge. Maybe everyone had correctly identified that my family was the most fucked up out of all of them. All of that was far above my ability to reason. We made our way to the grassy knoll and sat down at the top. We wore the same type of shoes. My Velcro straps stuck out at odd angles. Hers were neat and pink.

For the rest of recess, she talked to me about her parents and her home life. She told me about their fights and how scared she was when they happened. I remember her face—impossibly young for the caliber of emotions raging across her chubby cheeks and narrow nose. Her long brown hair was drawn up in a ponytail, clipped with a bright pink barrette that wagged as she shook her head from side to side. After some time, one of the teachers came over to check on us. Erin flatly told them what we were talking about. The teacher nodded and walked away.

I remember telling her that it was going to be hard but worth it. Two birthdays! Two Christmases! Oh right, she was Jewish. Well, two of those! She was going to have two rooms now, so she should keep a backpack with her favorite toys in it and take it to school with her on the days she switched houses. Oh, and having two rooms is great! Sort of. Well, maybe not really, but it would be for her. What were her favorite colors? Well, one room could be one color and the other could be another! It was going to be awesome!

My teachers told us often that lying was bad. I did it anyway. My kid brain couldn't comprehend that all parents weren't like mine. But she was my friend. I remember wanting to protect her the best I could.

The bell rang. We were supposed to head to the main doors for a head count. As the other kids ran around the corner to get in line, she started to cry. Heavy, wracking sobs shook her entire body. I sidled up closer to her and put my arm around her shoulder. One of the teachers poked her head around the pebbledash walls of the school—the same one that had checked on us earlier. She quickly disappeared again. Erin sobbed, her spit and snot leaving a huge puddle on my oversized T-shirt.

Soon enough, one of the student teachers came slowly out and sat on a nearby bench. She pointedly didn't look at us. The bell rang again and the sound of bustling kids died down as the heavy steel doors closed.

I have no idea how long we sat there. I never really paid attention to the bells in school. I was usually too tired. My teachers initially penalized me for tardiness, but soon stopped when they saw how much trouble I had staying awake in class. Eventually, it became one of those things that everyone ignored. A lot of time passed before she finished crying. I still had my arm around her. There we were: two starry-eyed kids with way too much to handle, hanging onto each other for dear life as the tides of life and time threatened to tear us apart, limb by limb.

When Erin finished, she grabbed my sleeve and blew the rest of her accumulated snot into the one remaining dry spot of my shirt. The student teacher must have been watching more closely than she let on because she was there in a flash, kneeling down and rubbing Erin's back. She flashed me a quick smile, said something about me getting back to class, then ushered Erin off toward the office.

I could lie and say that this was a watershed moment, that I stopped and appreciated the gravity of what had just happened, or that I had some epiphany. But that would be horseshit. I was a child.

I hopped and skipped across the painted concrete and slowly made my way to class, wondering whether I still had any candy stashed in my backpack. I did think about Erin during detention. I hoped she would want to play the next day.

3

THROUGH

Going to middle school was like jumping from a warm, bright feeder tank of goldfish to a massive, gray walled ocean tank of sharks and piranhas. The first day was an assault of names and superlatives that I had never heard before. My brother had laid the groundwork before I had even arrived. There was nothing he wouldn't say, nothing he wouldn't do, to make sure that I was universally despised. On my first day I was spat on, cussed at, and pushed against the wall. By the end of the first week, all of my t-shirts had tears and holes in them.

I had come into that school a scared kid just trying to make some friends. I quickly gave up. It was a losing battle that I had to survive. I remember counting minutes and hours as a way to pass the time. When I did have an assigned desk, I would carve sixty notches on the underside. Running my finger along the scoring and counting along with the clock on the wall became a repetitive exercise that calmed my nerves until the bell rang.

One day, as I walked out onto the concrete square for recess, I saw one of my brother's 'friends' going through his wallet and taking out all of the one-dollar bills I knew he kept hidden in it. My brother was shaking his head from side to side, not saying much. I ran over to the group and shoved one of them against the railing. But this wasn't elementary school anymore. These kids were a lot bigger than me. One sneered and punched me in the chest. Then it was a brawl.

It's strange, fighting four or five people at once. It becomes a guerrilla action. There is no thought in one's mind other than causing as much damage to as many people as possible. The thought of how many hits I was taking went completely out the window.

I got my ass kicked. But I managed to ram one of their fat heads into the thick metal railing, another I spun into a brick wall, and one even got an upper cut straight into his jaw. Me? Black eyes, bruises, the whole lot.

This was the start of a bi-weekly ritual. I was trapped in a vise that was slowly tightening, a tectonic plate's worth of force against me on all sides—including the sky. I remember looking at my brother after the scuffle was over. His eyes were pure, unadulterated hatred. It took a long time to understand that it wasn't directed at me.

I became well acquainted with the principals and detention in no time. I was making zero headway through a viscous current of hate and intolerance. I frequently ran into kids in the hall, where they would slap binders out of my hands, push me in the back, or throw punches as they passed. One day, it all became too much to bear.

I was outside when I heard my brother yelp. I dropped the basketball I was holding and turned. Two kids were holding my brother up by his armpits and shaking him. I snapped. Hands reached out from all directions, trying to slow me down, but my teeth were clenched. I made it over there in a full sprint and tackled the biggest, nastiest one of them. I felt his head hit the pavement—hard. His eyes went wide with surprise. I drove the underside of my palm into the flesh of his face just under his nose. He didn't move after that.

I immediately got up and turned to another, a rat-faced, skinny one wearing a Slayer T-shirt. I punched him as hard as I could in the stomach. I don't remember much about the rest, other than everyone was swinging.

There were more of them than me. Several teachers and both principals arrived. I kept punching. I wanted them dead. I repeatedly hit the teacher who was now holding me aloft in a bear hug.

Fuck 'em.

All of the adults were yelling simultaneously, their eyes shifting between me, my brother, and his friends. All five of them were dragged to the office. One of the teachers kneeled next to Tubby, who was still lying on the ground. I spat blood in that direction and sneered. The vice principal snapped twice at me, pointing toward his office. I looked at him, then glanced at the trail that led to my mother's house. For a moment, I considered giving it all up. I could just run…

A hand appeared on my arm and roughly jerked it forward. Away from the escape route, but also from the office. We walked along the back end of the school along a broad path of badly shattered concrete. Beneath us were the broad soccer and baseball fields that sloped down toward a group of apartment complexes in the distance.

It was October and the sun was shining, a rarity in the Pacific Northwest. The principal was a short man. A recent growth spurt had made me almost as tall as him. He carried himself as if he was much larger, with well-polished shoes and a well-tailored suit. His hair was immaculately oiled back over dark, deep-set eyes and a broad nose. He was usually very self-assured and confident. That day he just seemed tired. He put his hands in his pockets as he spoke. My fists were still balled up and I could taste the blood in my mouth.

We walked that way for the better part of the period, talking about the path I was on and where it would lead. I knew to listen to him. I was, at heart, a good kid. He told me that I wasn't going to be punished for this but that I should stop trying to protect my brother. He mentioned that he had figured this was going to happen as soon as I entered the school. Evidently, I had quite the 'permanent record.' He had been watching me.

I could barely hear what he was saying. My breathing was loud and ragged. Hate flowed through my veins like dextrose through an IV tube, pulsing and raging in time to my wrathful heart. They couldn't do this to us. They wouldn't do this to us. I would kill them if I had to... I remember stopping, looking up at the sun, then looking back at his face. He was staring at me with an odd expression. It was like he was curious and resigned at the same time. I had missed something important.

"You aren't listening to me, are you?"

I looked up at him with what I hoped was defiance. My legs shook like David's. My hands quivered like Ali's. I had a monumental choice to make, one that would change the entire course of my life. Of course, I didn't know that back then. But there didn't seem to be any choice at all. I was a kid. My life was one giant game of 'the floor is lava,' with no time-outs and no winners. It was survive or die. That was all I understood.

I chose wrong.

"Fuck you." I said, and walked away. I could hear him chuckling as I crossed under a covered entrance to one of the main halls. I was still shaking. The bell rang then, and hundreds of students piled out of the doors, flooding the hallway in a mass of bodies. I was close to my locker so I hurried over, grabbed my books, and scurried to my next class. For once, a wide swath appeared in the press of bodies around me. I must have looked quite the sight. I could see, however, Rat-Face staring above the door to his locker. He was smirking. Then he turned to grab something from inside...

I crossed the distance in an instant. It was as if time sped up to allow me to move faster. He had longer hair, which became really handy for me as

I grabbed a chunk of it and slammed his face into the metal shelf of the locker. I hadn't had enough though, so I did it again. And again. And again. Then, still breathing heavily, I high-tailed it up the corridor to make it to my next class. I could hear Rat-Face yelling behind me.

The rest of the day passed in an anxious blur. I had openly declared war and the next battle was going to be waged soon. I tried to focus on what the teachers were saying, but found it impossible. Ragged breaths punctuated the ticking clock, my fingers keeping pace on the notches underneath the desk.

There was no way out. I had just burned the last safe bridge off of an island full of rabid beasts. My fists clenched themselves, over and over, as if I could build enough strength in the next hour to be able to make a difference. I kept looking at my skinny arms, wondering how I was going to make them pay. It felt like waiting for the jailer to rattle her keys and let me out of my cage, with the abrasive touch of a noose around my neck, and the wobbly instability of a chair beneath my feet.

Luckily for me, there was a half-brother and sister pair that I was friends with. They were walking down the hall after my last class and must have gotten some kind of word. Ignoring the air of violence I was trying to project, they invited me over to their house to hide out until the whole thing blew over. They lived directly across the street. I wanted to fight. To the death if need be. They looked at each other, each one grabbing one of my arms. I tried my best to look fierce, rather than relieved.

As we passed the teachers directing traffic and ushering families out of the vestibule, my brother was standing there, looking around the rushing bodies. I dismissed it. I couldn't comprehend why he wouldn't love me the way that I loved him. We hurried past him, just three small kids bustling through the press. I didn't realize that I had been holding my breath until the door closed behind us.

We hung out for a while, doing homework and trading jokes. Before long, their parents came home, so I made for the door. The sun was setting. Dark clouds hung low in the sky, promising rain. A breeze picked up and carried the earthy smell of pine, oil, and damp that pervades the Northwest. I made it down the front steps before I saw them.

My brother was in front. He wasn't hard to miss, considering he was pointing right at me. Rat-Face was behind his bigger friends, a series of long and very red welts crossing his face. All of their eyes were glued. One was cracking his knuckles and grinning. My brother simply stood to the side and stared, his eyes blaring hatred and something else... as if he were confused about where he was. Or who he was. I knew how this was going to go. And sometimes in life, when everything is lost, there is nothing else for a man to do but charge.

I have never been afraid of pain. It had been ever-present in almost every facet of my life since my earliest memories. Maybe that is why I have always been a runner, a traveler, and a regular at the bar. I have always preferred to just get it over with. I could have outrun them easily. But that would be admitting fear and defeat. I rushed in, ducked an elbow, and put one right across Rat-Face's chin.

Rat-Face's open fist hit me across the left cheek. I knew it was coming and didn't try to dodge. That was as far as my plan had actually gotten. All I wanted was to land one really good blow; to make sure that these bastards knew who I was. My left hand was already sailing upwards. I caught his chin, moving upwards in what I hoped would be a deathblow. I wasn't strong enough. We both stumbled backward and the goons moved in. The last thing I remember clearly was seeing Rat-Face amongst the kicks and punches that they rained down onto my head, chest, legs, and arms. A smile crossed my lips. There was blood on his teeth.

I tried to get up multiple times, but the blows kept coming. Somebody was sitting on me now. Or were they kneeling? It didn't matter. I was enraged, spitting blood everywhere. I am grateful now that I didn't get up. I had a knife in my backpack and I was planning to use it. Eventually, they got tired and backed away, laughing. They turned and tried their best to look like they weren't running away.

There was still someone on me, harshly pushing me into the ground. I groaned and tried to spin. It was definitely a knee, right in the small of my back. I managed to get my head turned just enough to see it was my brother. His face was expressionless, rigid in a mask of indifference.

"Get the fuck OFF of me!" I bellowed. He got up quickly. I couldn't even look at him. I seethed under the heavy weight of his betrayal. I wanted to hit him, to make him bleed... But I knew that doing so would cause more problems at home. I started walking down the steps toward the school, hoping that I didn't run into anyone I knew along the way.

The way back to our mother's house was all uphill, a series of trails and winding streets that lanced across the steppes of the West Hills. The skies brooded and seethed. Without warning, the rain started to fall in thick, heavy swathes. Somewhere in the tussle, I had lost my sweatshirt. I consigned myself to the cold, raising my face to have my blood, sweat, tears, and the grime of pavement washed from my face. I felt nothing. I was an empty petri dish, limping home in the rapidly fading light.

When I got to the house, the lights were off, the doors were locked, and someone had forgotten to put the spare key back in the holder. My mother's car was in the driveway. I knocked a few times on the front door. There was no answer. I climbed through the front window, sliding the large pane gently across the tracks. It always made a screech and the harder you tried to do it quietly, the louder it was. My mother must have started awake at the sound.

"Hey, honey!" she yelled from upstairs. There was a noticeable slur to her words, as usual, but it was impossible to tell whether this was from her being asleep or something else.

"Hey, Mom."

"Did you have a good day?" she said, obviously content on staying where she was.

"It was fine."

I headed to the shower. My babysitter had taught me years ago how to wash out all of the various bumps, bruises, and cuts that a kid is bound to collect. The shower had become my safe place. I could hide in there, without the constant tension and fighting, where the warm water and steam would massage my shaking hands. I turned on the faucet, sat down under the stream, and gently rubbed my wounds until the water went cold.

In what had become a common theme, no one commented on the scratches, welts, or the black eye the next day. Or the day after. I was just a made-for-TV movie that someone couldn't be bothered to turn off. It never occurred to me to mention it to my mother. My brother ignored me completely.

For the next few months, school was a warzone. Every day brought a fight with someone else, usually someone I had never met. I avoided the bathrooms unless they were busy. I was a nervous wreck, constantly waiting for the next blow to come. When they invariably arrived, they came randomly, some kid sucker punching me from the side or slamming me with a full backpack. That never went well. I was determined not to be a pushover. I would either throw my books in their face or retaliate. Recess was a mixed bag. Either I was confronted by one of my brother's friends or nothing happened at all. My relationship with the principal evolved rapidly.

Then, something broke in my favor. By this point, I had two teachers who hated my guts. For what reason, I have no idea. I was a kid being a kid. The band teacher was the worst. She would mock me, in front of the entire class, for how badly I played my trumpet. She was the human equivalent of Jabba the Hutt, pounding diet cokes and constantly scowling. She had small, nasty eyes hidden in the rolls of fat on her face and thin, wispy hair that barely covered the scalp of her head. I didn't know how she had her job. Didn't any of these people know what monsters look like?

One day, in the middle of a song, nature called. I couldn't hold it, so I tore out of class without asking. I had made some friends by then. They never fought alongside me, but they seemed to care. One of them bolted after me.

When we returned, the band teacher was hollering about something that had been thrown at her. She blamed me. It was no use trying to convince her that it was physically impossible to have shot her with a spitball while I was crouched in a stall eight hundred feet and four sets of walls away. She was livid and embarrassed, so off I went to see my best pal.

I entered the office without waiting. He was leaning back in his chair with his hands behind his head. He didn't sit up as he asked about what had happened. I told him. I wanted to cry. The anxiety, constant violence, and general disrespect of everyone around me were one thing. Being belittled and openly disrespected by the very teachers that were supposed to be keeping me safe was something else. It was the knife in the darkness; the unseen cracks in the scaffolding. Apparently, the man in front of me saw it the same way.

With a jolt, he sat up and looked me straight in the eye for a long time. The silence stretched as we maintained eye contact. I could smell his cologne, aftershave, and pomade from across the expansive desk. The sharp white lighting cut into my tired eyes like a scalpel. Then he nodded.

"I'll do something about this," he said, motioning for me to leave. I sat there for a moment, stunned. What could he do? What could anyone possibly do? I was halfway through the door before he spoke again.

"Sam, take the rest of the week off."

It was Thursday. I made a beeline to my locker, my footsteps echoing down the long hallway. My books and backpack became the subject of my unexpressed emotions. They entered into their customary spots inside the metal cubicle with a fiery passion that guaranteed no homework would get done that weekend. I slammed the locker shut, kicked the outside door open with a foot, and ran home. I arrived just in time to catch the new episode of Pokémon. Thankfully, no one was there when I arrived.

Back then, we still had landline phones. This was 1999, before the craziness of Y2K, 9/11, The Iraq and Afghanistan wars, and the advent of mobile phones. Cell phones existed, but they were still too expensive. It was easier to get away with things then. When the school called to inform my mother of my latest infraction, you simply had to unplug the phone or answer quickly and hang up. The tricky thing was getting rid of a voicemail. It had a password on it that only my mother knew. The red light on the top of the phone would blink red, letting us know that someone had left a message. When I emerged from the basement, the light was blinking. I threw up my hands and waited for the worst.

But nothing happened. I sat and read a book in my room downstairs until nightfall, hearing the eventual arrival of both my brother and mother in their own time. No one came to talk. There was only the loud, purposeful hammering of footsteps and then... nothing. I couldn't believe my luck. I had dodged a bullet, for once, and lived to tell the tale. The confines of my room felt like a sanctuary. It was surreal. After a while though, I got hungry and left the safe confines to find sustenance.

Our basement was amazing for a lot of reasons, but primarily because it was far enough away from my mother's room upstairs that we could sneak in and out of the back door unnoticed. We would often invite our friends over on weekends and hang out in our basement without the parental control that these meetups usually required.

Despite it being a weekday, I came around the corner to see that they were all there. Rat-Face, Tubby, my brother, and three of the others were all sprawled across my couch like lichen clinging to the trunk of a gnarled tree. All of them stared at me with a heat and a passion that made my heart sink to my tailbone.

Oddly enough, the fear that had dominated my being for the past months was gone. In its stead was a desperate, gritty sense of being backed into the farthest, deepest corner of my mind. I could feel my psyche shifting into a fight-or-flight mentality, then orienting specifically to the 'fight' category. I'd had enough. This was my home and there was no way that these horrible monsters were going to threaten me here. I would kill them if I had to.

I walked by their hateful glances and went upstairs. The fridge was chock-full of sandwich-making supplies, likely the excess from one of my mother's open houses. I grabbed enough to feed an army—an entire platter of buns, charcuterie, and assorted cheeses. My mouth was watering from the smells of salt and grease that wafted from the crowded plate. I also grabbed the biggest, sharpest kitchen knife we had and placed it atop the pile.

Then I went downstairs. They were all still staring, the TV blaring with the noise of some cartoon. I walked straight toward them and spotted a six-inch divide between Rat-Face and Tubby. I put the tray in my left hand and the sharp knife in my right and plopped down between them.

I could feel the two of them writhing and wondering what to do next. Both of them lightly shoved me, but I ignored it. I put the tray of sandwiches across my lap, cut one sharply in half, and popped it in my mouth, saying something loudly about how much I loved the show that was on. I hated cartoons, even back then. But I didn't care. This was my couch.

Fuck 'em.

It only took a few minutes for the air to leave their sails. Rat-Face made a comment, but I 'accidentally' swung the knife toward his eyeball. They were there to intimidate me, to assert their dominance and make me submit. I am grateful that they tried. Because that was the moment when I decided to stop putting up with it. The gap widened as each of them realized what they had gotten themselves into.

Tubby tried to reach over and grab one of the sandwiches from the tray. I had been expecting this ever since I sat down. As soon as his hand crossed over the plate, I slammed the knife down, missing his skin by a fraction of an inch. It landed with a ringing crash. Rat-Face nearly jumped out of his skin. I smiled.

"Dang! Missed. Man," I said nonchalantly, "I *love* this show!"

Before the next commercial, all of them abruptly got up and shuffled toward the door. None of them looked at me this time aside from my brother. The hatred was still in his eyes, as if I had taken one of his Christmas presents and thrown it into the trash in front of him. I simply smiled and waved with my knife. I sat there and ate the rest of the sandwiches, turning the station to the news before the door had closed.

The rest of the weekend passed uneventfully. I didn't leave the house. My hands started shaking as soon as everyone left and never really stopped. I read a book and sat by myself, leaving my room only to take showers and eat. There was an impending sense of doom that covered everything. Victories in my life never seemed like victories. The other shoe was bound to drop soon. It was inevitable.

But it never did. I walked into the band room on Monday morning, my first class of the day, and was met with no insults, deprecating remarks, or any comments at all. Jabba simply read the announcements and carried on with the class. I was invisible. It was heaven.

The rest of the day went smoothly. There were no fights in the schoolyard, no sucker punches in the halls. The tremors in my hands slowly dissipated. The air contained oxygen again. It felt like taking my first breath of air after being held down in the deep end of the pool for so long.

Later that week, the principal gently waved me over as I passed by his office.

"How's it going?" he asked. His usually gruff demeanor was smoothed, kindness dripping out from the edges. He looked at me intently. Appraisingly.

"Fuck 'em," I said, brightly. I could still hear him laughing as I rounded the corner.

4

MYRTLE CREEK

I wasn't mad about getting slapped. If you call your mother a bitch enough times, it is bound to happen. What bothered me was that she would deny it. She loved violence in all of its forms. Whether she was too drunk, high, or self-righteous enough to remember what she had done was anyone's guess. But in my eyes, if you are going to hit someone, you damn well better mean to. And then, you need to stand by your decision.

Everything I cared about fit into a duffel bag. I was packed before the welt had faded from my face. I sat next to the small space heater in my room, listening to the rain and the engine idling in the driveway. Gentle rivulets of water ran down the window. The sound of tires slipping along the asphalt faded into the sounds of the city and everything stilled. A small speck of sun peeped through the clouds. I dressed quickly, swung the bag over my shoulder, and began to walk.

My father was recently divorced, and was lonely enough to want my company. It was midday when I arrived at his house. I found him sitting in the backyard after no one answered the front door. He already had the telltale signs of heavy drinking: red nose, flushed cheeks, and a sour bemusement dominated his face.

He was a brilliant man. His quick wit and incisive intellect were evident at all times, despite his irascibility. Today, he was all jokes, smiles, and firm handshakes. He handed me a BB gun and we set to work scaring off the neighborhood squirrels.

I shrugged off the drinking. That was just par for the course, the price of doing business with family. I still assumed that this was how parents were, and for the first time in my life, he was taking an interest in me. I would put up with a lot to keep that going. The scraps of love that were available to me were all I knew, so I greedily ate them up. There was something new, a foreign notion… was it hope? For the first time, I thought that I could get out of that town alive.

The feeling lasted for a few hours. I had been to the house before and picked out a room. The place was massive: three floors connected by two narrow, insulated staircases. There was enough room for the two of us to be physically separate at all times. This was clearly something he was used to. As I unpacked my bag and started to settle in, I called out to him. No one answered.

Around dusk, I got hungry and headed downstairs. He was in the kitchen, sitting in the same chair… at the same table… I went to the fridge, pulled out a soda, and cracked the can. It took me a moment to realize that I was holding my breath. I stared at the back of his head, gradually realizing that his entire body was shaking. He was sobbing.

Here was one of the twin pillars of menace in my life: a rollercoaster of guilt, hatred, and shame. It was impossible to predict who he would be at any given time. I'd learned long ago to constantly stay ahead of the tide, nose raised to the oncoming waves, both hands tightly gripping the rudder. Lapses in attention could lead to incorrect guesses, and those were dangerous.

But this was new. I had never seen him cry before. This was a moment of vulnerability, a tentative outpouring of nascent humanity, spilling over the vinyl floors of this glistening kitchen. I walked over to him. Slowly. Like you would a mewling tiger.

It took a few seconds to gain the courage. I put a hand on his shoulder. It seemed right. He started crying even harder, heavy, wracking sobs rippling through his body. He reached a hand backwards and put it over mine. The sunlight was coming in through the window, splaying out over the carefully laid tablecloth, one ray spearing directly into the bubbling glass of clear liquid he had been drinking from.

Suddenly, he turned and fell to the floor. I jumped backward, hesitating, thinking he was having a heart attack. The sobbing consumed him. He was grief personified, the small frame of his body barely able to contain his despair. He sunk his forehead to the kitchen floor. Small puddles formed underneath both of his eyes. I went to one knee and put a hand on his shoulder.

"Not so bad, Dad." I said. That was his favorite saying. He liked to repeat it in when he was in one of his better moods. To my surprise, my own voice sounded strong and purposeful. I was quickly shaking off the vocal tremors of adolescence. Still, with the tumult of the past month, I felt like crying too. It never occurred to me that this was inherently wrong, that I was offering the same type of consoling that I needed myself.

Slowly, his breathing returned to a normal rhythm. Fragments of sentences escaped. None of it made any sense, but I knew he had reached his limit. Two deep, shattered breaths broke through the patina, then he rose and, without saying a word, he went to his room. I heard a can crack shortly after.

The next three months flashed quickly. High school had just begun, a whirlwind of new faces and activities. At his insistence, I joined the football team. To him, that was right and correct. Young men, even the skinny, artistic ones, were supposed to play football. So, I did. For a week. It didn't take long before I had told the Head Coach to fuck off and was kicked off the team. I told no one and went to track practice instead. I would grab some spare pads from the locker room on the way out the door. As long as I was drenched in sweat, no one asked any questions. When I returned to his house he would lavish me with attention, insisting on going outside to play catch. For brief, illusory moments, it felt like home.

The days blurred together. Our nights were spent watching Blazer games, ordering pizzas, and reading Tom Clancy books. He was always one step out the door, moving from one room to another. It was difficult matching his activities. I tried hard though. Something in me knew that I had to make this time count. There were volatile moments. I learned quickly that when he left the house, he invariably returned in an unstable mood. He made a lot of noise on the stairs, which made him easy to dodge.

It all ended just as soon as it began. I was blinking sleep from my eyes and stuffing textbooks into my bag when he appeared in the doorway. He had a drink in his hand. With the bedside manner of a battlefield surgeon, he proceeded to tell me that he was moving. A ringing started in my ears. He rambled, on and on, about the lack of job opportunities, the women here, and how he needed a fresh start somewhere. It didn't seem real. He had just bought this house...

I knew what it all meant. I was fourteen. I couldn't get emancipated, couldn't get an official paycheck, couldn't get out of school... There was no escape. I was going to have to move back in with my mother.

My breath caught in my chest... Sharp talons gripped the outside of my heart. My vision tightened, narrowing, block spots dotting the outsides, pulling inwards, downwards, outwards—I could feel my hands tightening around the bag I held. He noticed none of this. He took a brazen sip of his drink and looked around the room as if seeing it for the first time. Maybe he was.

"Should've painted this white," He murmured. Then he turned on his heel and made his way down the stairs. I looked at my watch and realized I was late. I slung the backpack over my shoulder, slammed the front door, and sprinted down the street to the bus stop.

***

The morning was bitterly cold, with the pervasive chill that comes after a week-long rain. The moving truck was packed, the shiny new house emptied. My mother sat in her car down the street. My father walked over and looked at me with faded, yellow eyes. His gaze was discordant, as if it was darting between realities. He shook his head, then shook my hand. That was it.

My mother got out of the car and made a big scene of running over to me and giving me a hug. I knew that it was for show. I had embarrassed her, and now I was going to pay. I rolled my shoulders back reflexively, hands limp, staring at the new Lexus sitting there in the middle of the busy street. I crawled into the passenger seat, tucking my bag between my legs. The drive was mercifully short. I couldn't shake the feeling of being transferred to a more secure facility.

***

The school year was winding to a close when I next heard from my father. He wanted me to come and visit. Nothing seemed awry about this. I even had a friend, Aaron, who wanted to go with me. Somehow, we convinced his parents to drive us down.

I hadn't known that a four-hour drive could be fun. The family was singing along to the radio, playing road trip games, and bantering as we went.

This was a real family: healthy, united, and wholesome. I had never seen anything like it. The entire scene was a giant mirror illuminating everything that I lacked; that I wasn't. I could see in their faces that I was just as foreign. To me, this meant that I was deficient. Unworthy. It would never matter how polite or witty I could be. Eventually, they would figure out who I really was.

When they dropped us off, my father did his best to pretend he was sober, putting on his 'Responsible Dad' act. He was remarkably good at it. I could see the misgivings melting off of the faces of Aaron's parents. They slowly drifted back to the car, and they were gone. Aaron and I were on our own.

It didn't take long for him to be tired of us. Two hours from the time we had walked in the door, he suggested that Aaron and I go fishing. We were too excited to think clearly. He drove us to a spot on the way to town and left us there. I had brought nothing aside from a tackle box and two fishing poles. We were fifteen, though, bulletproof and confident. There was nothing to worry about.

After four hours, we had caught a reasonable string of trout. Aaron was a savant, and I was no slouch myself. Sunscreen hadn't made it onto our list of necessary supplies. The sun soaked deep, patiently taking its toll. Without noticing, we had become dehydrated, exhausted, and hungry. My father was nowhere to be found.

Aaron had a cell phone, so we began to make our way down the river, back toward the highway. After an hour, we took a break, watching the string of fish buck and swirl in an eddied pool below us, wondering if we could get away with drinking some of the river water… Luckily, Aaron and I had been lab partners in Biology together. We knew all about the kinds of things that swam around in river water. Our better senses prevailed. With no other options, we walked back to the highway and put out our thumbs.

Of all the miracles that could have happened at that moment, seeing my father was the last one I expected. But there he was. His immaculately polished white Cadillac pulled into the narrow turnaround right as we crested the hill. In typical fashion, my father took the initiative, rolling down the window and whistling at the sight of the long string of fish.

"Hot damn, boys! Now those are some *beauties*!" he exclaimed, grinning from ear to ear. His voice drawled slightly, catching on the vowels. There was spittle at the corner of his mouth.

And just like that, everything was brushed right out the window. This was how it had always been. Life, in all of its glory, dependent on nothing but the whimsies of tainted recollections. Everything changed on the briefest of breezes. The only thing that mattered was that moment. And that moment was completely separate from the rest of the day, regardless of what had happened previously. Delirious, we skipped towards him with glee. I tossed the pile of fish into the cooler in the trunk, threw open the side door, and jumped in just before he floored the accelerator.

When we got back to the house, it became very clear that my father had been at the bar all day. He was having a great deal of difficulty getting around the house. Aaron and I had sprinted in. We needed water, badly. After three or four large glasses, then a full can of soda apiece, we finally had enough energy to speak.

It didn't go well. Instead of Dr. Jekyll, we got Mr. Hyde, and this was Hyde at his absolute worst: mean, spiteful, and utterly unaware of both of those things. My father had officially stopped trying to be a parental figure. He had moved there to drink the way he wanted to drink. Now he was face-to-face with the one thing that should have been more important than anything else, the one element of his life that he couldn't run away from. His dark side had won. There was no more battle anymore. Just hate, spite, and self-loathing. I looked at his face and saw my mother staring back at me.

I knew how to handle him in this state. I acted excited, staring straight at Aaron, and asked him if he wanted to 'learn' how to gut the fish. He already knew, but we both also knew that he had to pretend otherwise. He went right along with it. We quickly made our way out to the garage and got to work. He was scared. I could tell by the way his knife kept slipping away. My hands were covered in scales and fish guts, but I reached out and grabbed his shoulder anyway. I did my best to sound calm and in control. My voice barely quivered.

"It's okay. He'll pass out soon. No matter what, you keep that phone on you, OK? I'll deal with him."

I was devastated, but there was nothing I could do. It is in these moments that a man can show no fear. The people relying on him cannot see him afraid, lest they start to panic. His enemies cannot either, lest they seek to press the advantage. You have only one option. You have to straighten up, hold your chin high, shoot for the best, and plan for the worst. I had gotten us into this mess, and I was going to have to get us out.

I could feel the fear. It was crouched in a thickly sloped closet, trembling underneath a thick, Teenage Mutant Ninja Turtles blanket... I pushed it away. Deep. Deeper. The naive optimism I often clung to meant nothing then. Until we were safe, I had to be the biggest man in the room.

Aaron poured ice onto the fillets and softly closed the lid of the cooler. I beckoned him to stay where he was. There was a landline in the garage, so I pointed to it. He nodded and then kept his eyes on the floor.

Crossing through the threshold from the garage into the main house was like stepping into a dream. My father sat in the kitchen, slouched against the same chair, a solitary pendant light gently swinging from the ceiling above. He must have hit it with his head at some point... There were two beers on the table. One was still unopened. I could see the moisture beading on the side, a small rivulet running down the glistening Budweiser label. He grunted slightly, grimaced, then leaned back with a smile pasted on his face and gestured toward the beer.

"Want a beer?" he asked, still smiling. I had never had one before. "C'mon. Have a beer with your old man."

I knew he would become angry if I refused. I sat down across from him and pulled out an identical chair to the one he sat in—one that had been in my nightmares for years. I was taking my seat at the table, the entire world of possibilities laid out before me, with one simple choice to make. One choice, infinite permutations. A world defined. I knew then, deep within my bones, that there was no right or wrong, that life was simply a series of choices that led to a series of outcomes. The flash of understanding exploded like a firecracker and was gone just as quickly. I grabbed the beer, twisted off the cap, and took a pull.

The man across from me was unfamiliar. The light around him buckled and waved, seemingly cast in the soupy miasma of a prehistoric swamp. From the murk and malaise, his bright white teeth gleamed. Then, his weight shifted to the right. He couldn't sit up straight. His head drooped towards his shoulder as he stared at me intently. The look he gave me was familiar. I'd seen it on my brother's face often enough.

It struck me how much bigger I was than him. He was 5 feet 6 inches at most. My mother was even shorter. My brother was somewhere around their height. Over the past year, I had shot up to over six feet. I also worked out a ton. I was a hulking figure next to him. Years later, it would come out that he didn't believe that I was his son. In that moment, it sure felt that way.

The seconds stretched into minutes. He was testing me. The machinations of his impressive mind were making convoluted assertions and grandiose assumptions. I could feel beads of sweat passing down the small of my back. I had to resist the urge to reach backward. Suddenly he rose, whisking himself out of his chair and quickly striding to his room. Goosebumps appeared on my arms and the hair on the back of my neck rose. I set the beer down. As the bedroom door closed, Aaron walked into the room.

For a brief moment, the fear returned. My gut was adamantly trying to make its way under the table. I could taste the bitter malt on my tongue. A cordless landline phone sat close to the bottle. It was one of the smaller versions that were colored and worked like a walkie-talkie. I slipped it in my pocket. Then my father, in all of his drunken glory, came out of his bedroom. He was carrying a rifle. I don't know why he had it. He wasn't even a gun person.

But there it was.

I can take no credit for what happened next. It certainly wasn't me. Something clicked into place over the young man who identified with my name. I stood up immediately, stepped in front of where Aaron was leaning against the wall, and rushed to my father. The barrel lowered slowly...

I will never know if he meant to do what he was doing, but there was no time to figure it out. I put one hand on his left arm and swung the barrel to the left with my right. I wasn't gentle. I was saying something soothing, trying to calm him, trying desperately to will this situation out of existence. He was easy to turn. Too easy. He ducked under me and thrust the rifle, barrel-first, toward my face. With the silence of infinity, I heard the click of the trigger being pulled.

Wait. I heard the trigger. How do you hear a trigger?

I grabbed the barrel and jerked it away from me, roughly pushing the man toward the bedroom. He flew back in a heap, hitting the door as he passed through the doorframe, making it bounce off the wall and rebound. I leaned forward, slammed it, and looked to Aaron.

"RUN!" I yelled. He stood motionless, frozen, then abruptly sprinted after me. I paused only to throw the rifle in the side closet, then we were out into the night.

The driveway was steep and led to a wide, open road in the nearly empty subdivision. This was Southern Oregon before it was cool, so my father's house had a virtually unimpeded view of the area nearby. There was a field across the street with a hill lining the other side and, beyond that, a tree line. Instincts kicked in. Aaron and I sprinted as fast as we could across the field, zigging and zagging until we got to the trees.

As soon as we were out of view, I pulled out the walkie-talkie phone. Amazingly, it worked. God bless those marvels of engineering. I dialed 911. The voice on the other end was terse and uninterested. I screamed into the phone:

"MOTHERFUCKER HAS A GUN AND TRIED TO USE IT!!!"

That got her attention. I didn't wait for her reply. The phone had a locator function where it would beep if you pressed a button on the home terminal. My father knew this, as this was how he always located his phone when he was drinking. I tossed it as far as I could. Then we sprinted for the other side of the tree line. After a short while, I heard the phone start chirping behind us.

When we stopped, we were both out of breath. Aaron was white as a sheet, shivering in the cold. I couldn't have looked much better. We were both in shorts and t-shirts, and the temperature had plummeted as soon as the sun went down. I felt something wet on my foot. I looked down and realized that I wasn't wearing any shoes. I had also cut myself badly, somewhere in the field.

There we were, two skinny, hungry teenagers, freezing cold and standing in a small-town field, scared out of our wits. And out of nowhere, it became funny. Really, really funny. Too funny.

I had heard the trigger.

I looked up at the stars, laughing. Aaron stared, no doubt wondering if I was cracking up. I was taught later that some of us have that reaction in moments of intense stress. My brain had learned how to compartmentalize and adapt. Hopeless, impossibly fucked-up situations had become my comfort zone. And when there is nothing sane, healthy, or worth living for in a given moment, humor is the brain's last resort to protect itself. I knew I was making it worse for Aaron. I tried to stifle the laughter and couldn't.

Within minutes, a cop car came blaring toward us, popping over the small knolls and hillocks of the field, the engine roaring. I have never been a huge fan of police cars, especially not at that age, but in that moment, that Crown Victoria was a golden chariot storming across the river delta, parting the tides of bloodthirsty barbarians, here to save us from the gaping jaws of fate.

The cop pulled over and jumped out. He was in plain clothes, a button-up shirt tucked into loose-fitting slacks. The badge hanging from his neck looked real enough. We ran to him. As we neared, he opened the back door. Like stuntmen, we dove through the opening, piling atop one another. It took a few seconds to arrange ourselves on the slippery plastic bench. Despite the thick bars between us and the front seat, I felt safe. Kind of. I tried hard not to giggle. It was a losing battle.

As he drove us to the station, he told us that my father had called. He had said that we were 'up to no good.' I looked down at my bare feet, covered in dirt and rotting leaves. I could feel blood seeping onto the sticky plastic floor. It occurred to me to make some kind of remark, but nothing came to mind. I saw Aaron start to recede, pulling within himself. This was clearly his first time in the back of a cop car. Something tickled—the same sense I had gotten earlier… something, older. I realized that I had to sit up straighter. Brushing off my knees, I reached toward the bars and tried to make jokes with the cop. He could tell what I was doing and played along. Aaron didn't laugh much. We kept trying.

The next few hours were a blur. We had to wait in the police station for Aaron's parents to drive back. We spent the time spinning in office chairs and practicing our form on the small putting green that had been set up in the break room. At some point, a female officer came in and dressed the cut on my foot. As she did, I turned to Aaron and smiled. The color had returned to his face.

When Aaron's parents were fifteen minutes away, the cops drove us back to my father's house. There were three squad cars in total. I could see him in the driveway as we drove up. A gorge rose in my throat. Two officers guided us through the house, and two more escorted my father behind the garage. Aaron and I darted in the open door, rapidly tossed things into our backpacks, and bolted back out. We ran across the same driveway we had fled down hours before. Each step felt like a long dream. Adrenaline fatigue was starting to set in. As we reached the street, Aaron's parents pulled in the driveway. They didn't get out of the car.

His entire family had come. His mother was driving and insisted that I sit up front with her. Aaron huddled in the back with his father and all of his siblings. As the car turned the corner, away from the cookie-cutter neighborhood, past the field we had stood in, I could hear the mass of bodies shift. I looked over my shoulder and saw Aaron's father whispering urgently in his ear, holding his son tightly. I could feel someone's leg rhythmically pulsing on the seat behind me. Aaron was lost in a sea of arms, all clutching, holding...

I had heard the trigger.

I tried to speak, to make light of everything. I knew that Aaron's mother must be exhausted. It was my duty to keep her entertained... but nothing came out. All I could do was stare ahead. As soon as we hit the highway, my hands started shaking. Aaron's mother reached over and grabbed my arm, squeezing tightly. Not letting go. At some point, exhaustion must have set in. I drifted off to the rhythm of the freeway.

I awoke with my head between my knees. We were at my mother's house. The bright light of morning was glaring. I looked over, and Aaron's mother was staring at me with a tired face. I stared at the house for a moment, then turned to the backseat where Aaron and his siblings were still sleeping.

"I am so sor-" I started to say.

"Don't you *dare* say this was your fault," she cut in. Her face held a twinge of anger, yet she was doing her best to force a terse smile. Then she softened, grabbed my hand, and gave it a squeeze. "Don't you dare!"

But it was my fault. I knew it. It was a truth as inseparable from my being as breathing. I had put Aaron in that situation. I had poked the beast. It was absolutely my fault. Everything was. My mother, my father, my brother... all of them... I couldn't save any of them. They would have been happy if it weren't for me. If I hadn't been born. They would've been able to...

Aaron's mother was still staring at me. There was no telling how long the silence had stretched. I blinked twice and said nothing. Somehow, the car door opened. I went to the trunk, grabbed my backpack, and stood there waving to the car as it pulled away. As if I had just been dropped off after a weekend at the beach. Or summer camp. Walking back into my mother's house was surreal. No one was home. I felt like a ghost, haunting an abandoned ruin. I felt like an alien, stranded on a world without sunlight or oxygen. I went straight to my room, collapsed into bed with my clothes still on, and slept for the rest of the day.

Later that evening, when my brother and mother did return, neither asked me why I was home early. I don't think either of them had registered that I was gone in the first place. No one ever asked why my right foot was wrapped in a thick bandage either. No one asked a damn thing at all.

Sometime later that night, I crept from my room. My foot dragged a little, but I knew the creaky spots in the floor to avoid. I could hear snoring coming from upstairs. I slunk to the closet and rifled through my mother's coats. I knew there was... bingo!

I held the crumpled pack of cigarettes aloft and gently pulled one out. There was a lighter too. I snuck out the back door, through the blooming garden, and sat on a wooden bench in the middle. At my feet were creeping orange flowers, wilted in the night's chill, brushing at my ankles with grainy insistence. I lit the cigarette and took a drag. It felt good, everything considered.

I never spoke to Aaron again.

5

HOOKY

Plates rattled on the lacquered wood counter as she roared up the driveway. She had bought herself a Jaguar. It was an ostentatious beast, good for only one purpose: making an impression. The engine sounded like a cross between a cat's growl and a 747. Every time I heard it, the muscles in my forehead and shoulders tensed. Bracing. I was definitely impressed.

There were a lot of people still in the house. My mother was rarely home. She was either working, out at the bar, on vacation somewhere, or a mix of all three. We had quickly learned that we could get away with anything as long as the house was clean when she did show up. Even then, everything was dependent on how sober she was.

Luckily, I'd followed my normal routine: up with the sun to scrub the floors and countertops, remove all of the evidence, pile the garbage bags by the back door. Coffee percolated down into the pot. The sound reminded me of a plastic man clearing his throat. I was cooking breakfast for the troops. I knew what they liked to eat. Most had risen from their favorite spots on my basement floor. I could hear rustling down the narrow hallway from the one who preferred to stay in my room.

Bodies pressed against my back, milling, pulling food straight from the pan. Most of the coffee went straight into cups held by trembling hands.

I pushed down the rush of panic, picturing her fury at finding out, the consequences her wrath might have on the shards of my freedom...

I quickly ushered all of them toward where I slept. Luckily, the girl had dressed quickly. As soon as the last bewildered body ducked into my musty room, I slammed the door and slipped back into the kitchen. A pancake was just starting to smoke. I rammed a spatula underneath it and flipped. Batter sprayed across the tan, roughly hewn tiles.

As the keys hit the latch, I was furiously shoveling eggs and pancakes into my mouth. I had made a lot of food. Some of it had to disappear. The first insults left her mouth before the front door was closed. It never mattered how good my grades were or how many activities I participated in. Nothing could change her perspective, and I was the only one left around who was willing to take her abuse, to gobble up the scraps of love that she occasionally doled out. I stood there and took the punishment.

I choked back my replies, acutely aware of how many ears were listening. Whiffs of vodka cut through her typical odor of smoke, perfume, and fine dining. Her clothes, usually immaculate, were ruffled, with dust stains on the cuffs. She stared at me from across the room, rheumy, bloodshot eyes set back in an exhausted face. Her jaw was set with something immutable and unmovable, an ancient pain directed outward.

I was used to the constant verbal assault. Her words were emasculating scythes that slowly eroded my self-esteem and built dependence on her. I knew nothing else. This was how parents were. Love was cutting someone down enough times that they grew back indomitable. It was almost genetic, a family tradition passed down through countless generations. She ranted, raved, and spit. I wondered how she even had the energy to be so nasty. I could barely lift my head.

A half-hour had passed when she stopped abruptly, remembering something. With a sharp twist, she turned on her heel and darted back out the door. The engine roared back to life and rapidly pulled away. She had left her metallic mug, her constant companion, on the kitchen table. I opened it, thinking there might be some coffee left. Instead, ice cubes rattled loudly and the smell of sour grapes wafted up towards my nostrils.

Don't mind if I do...

I downed the container, then hollered at my guests. They poured from the room. All eyes were on the remaining pile of food. They ate quietly, their faces abashed. I never talked about my parents. No one had made much of an effort to find out more. We had left it at that. It couldn't be ignored this time. I looked at the pile of pancakes and eggs, then offered them seconds, thirds, and coffee refills. Most declined.

My closest friend took a bite of my pancake, and then gave me a long, deep hug. His beard tickled the side of my neck. I could feel the emotions start to bulge and bubble upwards. I tried to pull away. He gripped tighter. Then another piled on.

Soon, I was immersed in a huge puddle of arms and bodies, undulating in concentric circles in the middle of the kitchen. Coffee burbled in the pot, clearing its plastic throat. Warmth spread, gripping tightly as it folded in. I'd gone numb. Something in my mind couldn't connect, as if someone had spliced an internal circuit and forgotten to reroute it back to the mainframe. Warmth began to seep through the chinks in my armor. No one said a word.

An alarm went off. Duty called. The menagerie slung their backpacks across their shoulders and darted out the front door to the bus stop. One stopped before leaving and shot me a questioning look. I shook my head. As he closed the door behind him, the girl sidled up underneath my arm.

"Want to stay in bed today?" she whispered. I looked down at the counter. A small dollop of syrup that had been clinging to the edge slowly dripped onto the floor. I could feel the redness creeping up my neck toward my cheeks. The knuckles of my hands were white, bones jutting out at strange angles...

I didn't know what I wanted. I couldn't feel, couldn't see. I knew there was something I needed to do about... this. Something I needed to wrap my head around. But it was too much. I slipped down, down, down into the void. The weight of her thin frame pressed against me. Casually. Invitingly. I said nothing as she slipped her hand into mine and led me back to my room.

6

'Camp'

"...please get in the car. Sam. You need to..."

"I don't need to do shit," I said and started to put my headphones back on. She'd found me. After months of couch surfing, I'd made the fatal error of walking along the road near her house. I picked up the pace. Maybe one of my jobs would let me pick up an extra shift.

"Sam, I am *sorry*, okay? I am..." I didn't hear the rest. My mother had never apologized to me. Ever. It stopped me in my tracks. She was still speaking.

"...have you been? I've been worried sick..."

That's the alcohol.

"...heard you have a job? I didn't know that..."

Two, actually.

"...well, I think you're going to need a phone. Do you want a cell phone?"

Damnit.

That would make my life infinitely easier. I stared at her, feeling nothing. Surely I should have felt something. Right? A cell phone though...

I got in the car.

***

I woke up the next day to two men standing in my room. They didn't bother to hide the firearms attached to their hips. They had stormed in, slamming open the door, as if I had done something wrong. These men were clearly there to take me somewhere.

"Get up," the shorter one demanded.

"Get the fuck up!" said the other.

I took my time, knowing I was cooked. I also knew that I had been betrayed. This became very evident when the two men started screaming at me to drop my weapon.

I had no idea what they were talking about. I have always slept naked, so there was nothing in my pockets. As I looked down, it dawned on me that I had a knife in my hand. I was also in a half-crouch, with the blade facing backwards. Combat stance. These goons clearly recognized it. One had unclipped the gun at his side and had his hand hovering over it. The knife clattered as it hit the floor.

The two men led me out by the arms to the living room. My mother was standing there, bleary-eyed and clearly still intoxicated. She held tightly to her victimhood like a warming blanket after a long swim in the ocean. She started to say something, but I cut her off.

"Fucking liar."

A few hours later, I was being admitted into a wilderness rehab program. To add to the ignominy of getting abducted, they had me strip naked, crouch down with my butt cheeks and legs open, then rotate in a circle three times. Two men watched the show. They claimed that they were checking for drugs and alcohol. I stared at them intently the entire time.

Years later, this place, and a host of others like it, would all be shut down for gross human rights violations.

I found myself at a group meeting. My mother and brother showed up late. There were forty people in a circle, including my fellow inmates and their families. I was the only one who sat alone. The other parents tearfully gave long speeches about their children's behavior and what they hoped the kids would achieve there.

On my end, one of my parents hadn't bothered to show up, and the other, clearly drunk, said that she had forgotten to put anything together. My brother just stared. When pressed to speak, both of them blamed me for behavior that sounded a lot like their own. As my brother went into detail about how I was the reason he smoked so much marijuana, I slipped into numbness.

When it was my turn to talk, I told the truth. For the first time, I spoke openly about my life. I told the circle about my mother's behavior, the recent experience with my father, and my life at school. When I looked up from the floor, most of the other parents were staring at me with concern. Certainly, all of the moms. Except mine that is. She was angrily staring at the ceiling.

The meeting concluded abruptly. Families stood there, hugging and crying, holding and clinging. I walked to the door and asked to be let out. This was going to be the new normal. So be it.

Just get me away from these people.

Mercifully, we were shortly whisked off and packed into a van. The drive was five hours long and completed in total silence. Another new rule. No talking, unless approved by a staff member.

The ancient van creaked and moaned, along with some of the other kids who were already starting to go through withdrawals. I thought back to the rides to the beach with my father. I knew I wouldn't be having any pie on this trip.

Somewhere deep in the night, we pulled off a poorly maintained dirt road onto a trailhead. Stars perforated the pitch-black sky. Icy gusts wormed under my sweater, assaulting each pore individually. I figured there had to be some kind of cold weather gear for us. But I couldn't ask. Instead, I stood and waited.

As I looked upward, staring at the Milky Way above, someone rammed a 50-pound pack against my chest and a headlamp in my hand. I was then 'instructed' to start hiking. I didn't argue. What was the use? More hours passed. My pack fit poorly on my back, clearly not meant for such a lengthy torso. The chafing was intense. My muscles ached from the strain.

Finally, we were told to stop. It was time to set up our tents. We had been assigned a tarp and a walking stick for this purpose. I figured it was around 2 am. One of the counselors, a tall woman with blonde dreads and a passionate hatred for anything masculine, came over to me to 'help.'

Her aid consisted of pulling out a piece of paper with instructions on it. There were diagrams showing eight different types of shelters that could be made with just a tarp. She threw it on the ground at my feet, then walked away. It took me an hour after that to finally get something resembling a shelter. By this point, it was pouring down rain. I still couldn't find a sweatshirt.

Sleep was slow coming. I tossed and turned in my sleeping bag. I had been so close. I had worked and saved, skipping classes that I didn't need to take to pick up extra shifts. I'd paid a lawyer to start an emancipation case. A friend of a friend had an in-law unit they would rent to me in cash, so long as I maintained my jobs and my grades… They woke us up a few hours after dawn and screamed at anyone who was 'late' breaking camp. Then, we hiked the rest of the day.

The next two weeks were defined by quiet desperation. Most days consisted of a hike of at least ten miles through rugged terrain. On our days off, we did trail maintenance and heavy labor. We weren't allowed to talk outside of mealtimes and 'therapy' appointments. The staff had no such restrictions, and peppered me with 'advice' and 'wisdom' that sounded a lot like poorly concealed ridicule and abuse.

At no point were we allowed to bathe. Our boots were taken away at night, to keep us from running away. They were also determined to prevent suicides at all costs. So, naturally, we couldn't have any metal. To eat our meals, we were urged to make our own utensils out of wood, carving out hollow indentations with sharp rocks. It was either that, or eat with your hands. Some kids did.

One morning found us camped in a broad bowl, a divot carved into the top of a high ridgeline. Fog hung low, caressing the dew that still clung to the ground. My bare feet rested on the rocky soil, pine needles wedged between several toes. Today was special, evidently. Usually there was some kind of bell, whistle, or abrasive call sometime around dawn. I'd awoken that day on my own accord, dim light crawling underneath the taut edges of my shelter.

I crawled out and made a quick cup of coffee. At least they allowed us that. A blanket-swaddled mass appeared. It was Jay, the eldest member of the staff. In his hand he held a plate full of pancakes, eggs, cheese, and some kind of jerky sausage. He smiled broadly as I slurped the drool from the edge of my mouth and pointed at myself. He nodded and sunk down to a crouch. He'd brought me a real fork.

Jay and I had become close. I wasn't comfortable talking to anyone else. When some of the other inmates threw tantrums on the trail, or refused to do their work at all, he would usually appear at my side and point up the trail. The two of us, and a few other dedicated inmates, moved through the line and continued on. We usually got to camp a few hours ahead of the main group.

As soon as I was finished, he took the plate and precious metal and ushered me away. The center of camp was a boulder-strewn clearing with two stunted, gnarled trees growing in convergent directions. They each held multiple limbs toward one another, firmly reaching out... grasping...

A set of tarps was draped from the hardwood limbs and tied to small, lichen-covered boulders. Someone had built a fire. The wood was wet and produced smoke that escaped from a small hole between the edges of the tarps.

Jay returned, putting a hand on my shoulder and a large cup of coffee in my hand. I took a giant sip. It was regular, brewed coffee. A miracle. The smell alone left me lightheaded. Intoxicated. By now, the food and coffee had me wary. I took another large slug from the mug as he sharply inhaled.

"You're not going to be able to push through this," he said. I stayed silent, wondering what the hell that meant. I looked toward him, searchingly, but he stared straight ahead. He gestured forward.

"Get yourself a seat close to the fire. It's going to rain today," he said. His voice sounded strained, as if he were gritting his teeth through pain. "Want some more coffee?"

I nodded and sat beside the small but intrepid fire, surrounded by fellow inmates and staff members in a loose circle. The reason for the special treatment became apparent soon enough. That day was going to be a group meeting where we were going to read the letters that our parents had sent and discuss what we had done to land there. It was going to take all day, they insisted, so we should settle in for the long haul. I had picked the spot closest to the fire, my back to the largest of the small boulders. I closed my eyes and braced myself for what my parents had to say.

The time estimate was accurate. There were twelve of us, and most of the parents were eloquent. Every letter had to be read, discussed, and then opined about by everyone in attendance. It was the first time in two weeks that we were allowed to have open conversation with one another. Most of it was highly constructive. The majority of us had bonded strongly, coming together through a shared sense of adventure and grim defiance.

After eleven rounds of this, the sun was starting to set behind the trees. Rain had come and gone. Water still hung heavy in the air, and dark pillows of clouds rolled through the clearing at random intervals. I had read countless imaginary letters by then, imagining the words, the concern, the vitriol... Now that everyone else had finished, there was no hiding from it; it was time to hear it. I held my breath and waited.

Nothing happened. The guides shuffled awkwardly for a few moments and everyone looked at me expectantly, waiting for me to read. One of the other inmates even nudged me on the arm. I looked at him, then at the guides. They hadn't handed me anything.

"Damn it, fine. I'll do it," Jay exclaimed. He rolled to one knee and dug into the bag near where the food was kept. After a minute or so of rummaging, he pulled something out, turned to me, and slapped a piece of paper in my hand.

It was a postcard. I stared at it in disbelief. All of the other kids had read at least twenty pages—some even more than that. Handwritten, detailed, and delineated. Events, references, and patterns. Everything that the parents had noticed about their children and their maladaptive behaviors.

Mine was a solitary piece of paper. A postcard with a picture of Crater Lake. It was from my father.

> Hope you're having fun at camp! - Beck

I sat in stunned silence. A postcard. As if this was summer camp and I was grilling hot dogs, jumping in the lake, and flirting with girls, rather than deadlifting the problems of my entire ancestral line. There was nothing about how he had been a complete failure as a parent, or any kind of apology for trying to kill me. Instead, I had received the starkest of reminders that he knew nothing about my life and simply didn't care.

My mother hadn't sent anything at all. A flash of rage blossomed deep within, a nascent nucleus of awareness that instantly became the driving force behind all of my decisions. I sat cross-legged, deep in the wilderness, staring deep into the fire ahead, feeling the magma bursting from the core.

Just as the wood knows that it is not going to escape the flames below, I knew. I could never again live under the delusion of thinking that these people cared, that I would ever have a place in their aberrant hierarchy. I was on my own.

It had started to rain again. Thin sprays of water drifted across my lap.

To these people, I was just an angry problem to be swept to the side. I was the one who wouldn't fall in line, who refused to accept the generational status quo. Generations of dysfunction and coping strategies had resulted in... me. Sitting there, a lanky child, handling all of their problems. I saw them for what they were. And this terrified them.

Someone was speaking. They went on about how all the parents had been strictly informed that this was necessary, that this was a critical component of the entire process. Supposedly, they weren't allowed to enroll us in the program if they didn't agree to write something. Jay looked at me intently as the other spoke. Something was wrong with my vision though. I couldn't see anything.

Soon, everyone was staring. I tried to say something and couldn't. I tried again. All that came out were snatches of words and guttural noises, quickly replaced by heaving breaths. I started sobbing. My shoulders wracked in heavy, thunderous beats, as water poured from my face, all in silence. The rain intensified, battering the tarps above. The other members of the circle crowded in toward the fire, away from the onslaught. Someone threw the remaining wood on the fire.

I don't know how long I cried for. Every few minutes or so, I tried to say something, but was overcome by another fit. I was just a scared, fifteen-year-old kid, in the middle of nowhere, getting yelled at and abused in a mockery of drug and alcohol rehabilitation, completely alone. There was nowhere to go home to. There never had been. I pawed at the dirt, digging deep into the packed soil. I could feel the blood seeping from my fingernails. My father's words echoed in my head.

Not so bad, Dad.

The rain had let up and the sun was setting when I came back. For the first time, I looked up at the other faces in the circle. Aside from the blond woman with dreads, all of them were sobbing. Heat from the blazing fire had seared a patch of dry Earth on the ground between us all. I still couldn't breathe. Aftershock spasms jolted through my spinal column. I tried to stand and fell to my knees.

All of the other inmates sprang upwards. Of course, touching each other was strictly forbidden. This time, no one said a thing. There was one girl in the group. She reached me first and tackled me to the ground, wrapping her arms around my chest, squeezing my ribs. Other hands came in, holding my shoulder, my head, my arms, my hands... I was wrapped in a maze of human limbs. I fell then, deep into the abyss.

My clothes were waterlogged when I rose to my feet through the pulsing mass and staggered forward. The fire had died down, leaving heavy plumes of smoke that swirled in random directions. One of the staff members instructed us to return to our tents for an hour of reflection. I stayed where I was. There was nothing to reflect on. As soon as the others cleared out, I turned to Jay and requested my bow-drill kit.

There were levels to complete in the program, each with its own freedoms and luxuries associated with it. I had climbed through them quickly and stalled when it came time to bow-drill a fire. It was where most inmates gave up, evidently. It is not an easy task. You have to find a rock with a smooth divot, a spindle that is straight and will rotate rapidly, then craft a bow that isn't too firm yet won't snap under the pressure. Then you have to use them to make a fire. Jay handed these to me and crouched down.

"Smooth and steady," he whispered.

I could hear the rest of the staff bustling behind me. The darkness grew rapidly as the last waning threads of daylight desperately shot through the thick forest around us. I held the spindle down with my rock and rhythmically pushed and pulled the bow. I felt the frantic need inside me to cover it all up, to produce something, to succeed. I had to find an ember, a light at the end of the tunnel. I kept at it, drilling hole after hole into the nurse log. I could sense the impatience behind me...

Smoke appeared.

Jay whooped and thrust a handful of brush into my hands. I rapidly curled it into a ball, punching a pocket into the middle like he had shown me. And carefully, like a surgeon removing shrapnel from a wound, I tilted the jagged board over the waiting ball of tinder. The burning ember hesitated, then fell. With the ball of brush cradled in my hands, I blew gently, softly, insistently... until it burst into flames. All of the staff members were hollering now, loud exultations that drew my fellow inmates out from their tents.

We sat around that fire deep into the night. Nobody said much. When the time came to retire to our tents, I handed my boots to the nearest staff member and threw the last of the wood onto the fire.

I awoke early the next morning to the sound of birds. The fog had lifted. Sunlight shone brightly on the fat drops of water that clung to every available surface. Jay sat nearby. As I began to stir, he approached, a steaming cup of coffee held out in my direction. His smile was as broad as the ridgeline we were camped upon.

The next four weeks were a blur of shitting in the woods, long hikes through the mountains, and the beginning of a deep love affair with the wilderness. One day, we passed along a divided ridgeline. To the right of the winding trail were a jagged collection of white stones and stunted trees. To our left was a steep drop off. A fall would be instant death. I was last in line that day, right behind an inmate that I called Pudge.

The boy was a mindless wreck, incapable of almost everything—a blob of complaints and self-pity. He kept peeking over the edge, softly whining, and then hitching his way a few more steps up the trail. Every few feet, he stumbled, but it wasn't accidental. I had been watching him closely. He had been gradually slowing down over the past twenty minutes and now he was barely lifting his feet above the ground. This put us both in danger. But Pudge had decided, most likely hours before, that he didn't care. Eventually he 'fell,' letting his weight tumble towards the ground. But not forward—backward. Onto me.

Despite the weight of my pack and my own fatigue, I caught him as he flopped onto me. The sheer force of his bulk drove me back, twisting my ankles in directions they weren't supposed to go. I couldn't let go. The only thing that kept us both from falling to our deaths was the strength of my arms and hands, now holding him up by the straps of his pack. As soon as his momentum slowed, I roughly threw him to the ground, toward the slope above. He started squealing and crying as if I'd struck him. I didn't care. I went off.

I screamed in his face, anger and hatred flowing out of me in a fiery tornado of pure blackness. Something from deep within rent itself free, a tear appearing in the placid mask I had developed.

A staff member called for silence, so I screamed at them too. No one could get to us. The trail was too narrow to move anyone out of the way safely. I kicked the poor creature in the legs, then moved forward and screamed in his face. I went off about how he could have killed me, how he was constantly a burden, how hard I tried to get him to love me, how unfair it was that he couldn't just be a fucking adult and let me go...

I screamed that I didn't deserve this, that I had nowhere to go. That I was done with being saddled with incapable, pathetic, self-obsessed people. That I was the one who wanted to jump off the side of that cliff... the one who needed a fucking hand...

I was on my knees again. Pudge had drawn himself up against the mountain, eyes wide, breathing deeply, his tears replaced by raw terror. I glanced over and saw that the line of people had moved far ahead. Every head was turned, staring with a mixture of amusement and irritation.

From somewhere, Jay appeared at my side. I felt his hand on my shoulder first. I was gripping the ground again, churning the dirt and rocks together with both fists, blood rising up my fingers in deep lines, reaching up to meet the tears and snot running down my face. He whispered quiet, soothing phrases, gently pulling me upward and away. I let myself be led. The entire line moved as far upslope as they could while we passed.

Behind me, I heard another member of the staff call out to the rest of the group, announcing lunch time. There was a collective sigh, a few groans, and the dull, heavy thud of packs hitting the ground. We dodged countless rocks and crooked roots as we made our way up the winding trail.

"I don't think you're the problem," he finally said. The words were flat, uttered without emotion, yet they seared into my brain like a brand onto the flesh of a fuming, writhing bull. He expounded on this, talking about things that I shouldn't have known about. He told me about the inner workings of the program, how the parents were supposed to contribute and support us while they were there, and how mine were the first ones in the history of the program to adamantly refuse. He told me about my psychological evaluations and those that had been conducted on my family. When he talked about my mother, he used the word 'narcissism' often. He asked me if I knew what it meant.

"I think she wanted to get rid of you," he added, taking his sunglasses off and polishing them on his shirt. Heavy limbs waved behind his head. Insects buzzed and harried, darting between them. I stared at him until, suddenly, I popped like an over-pressured bag of chips. My entire life gushed out of me. I told him what I could remember from when I was young, my life at school, and my relationship with my family. He listened intently until I was done.

Then we dissected it, pulling it apart in thin strips of understanding. For the first time, I saw my role in my own life. He pushed me to see it—to take accountability—even for things that I had no business apologizing for. I finally saw that I wasn't a kid anymore. I hadn't been for a long time.

"You can either accept that or start to face serious consequences," he warned.

"What, like this shit?"

"No swearing," he said, stifling a grin.

"Sorry."

"I see..." he started, but held back. His head turned toward the sky. The heat was soothed by intermittent gusts of wind, whistling through the surrounding wilderness.

"I see how hard you try," he said, finally. "But a judge won't."

Before I had a chance to reply, another staff member came into view, swiftly moving across the switchbacks, three other inmates in tow. All of them were staring at me, concern plastered on their faces. Jay looked back at them, then turned to me.

"Do you want to do something fun?" he asked, looking upslope. Something jutted, just out of view—a peak of some kind.

Of course I did. The last two months had been torturous. The idea of levity was a foreign concept. The others were about to catch up to us and they were all smiling. Evidently, they had the same idea as Jay. Suddenly, it hit me: we were going to race.

As soon as the group reached us, we all threw our packs to the side, grabbed a water bottle, and took off up the hillside. The trail quickly disappeared, replaced with sharp cutbacks across a thick scree field lined with massive ledges of stone. Two of the other inmates veered left and started to zig and zag. I went straight up.

I don't think you're the problem, Sam.

A giant weight had been lifted from my soul. Someone had heard me. Seen me. Countless emotions that I couldn't process poured out through my hands and feet as I gripped massive stones. I threw myself forward. Upward. The hand holds came reflexively and naturally; the mountain below an extension of my arms. I lost track of time, place, and the people around me.

I reached the top breathless and smeared in sweat. Jay and another inmate appeared seconds later. If there had been a big red button to smash when we got up there, it would have been a photo finish. I knew that they had let me win. No one spoke. The expanse before us was vast, a sweeping canvas of immaculate brush strokes. The sun beamed down as a thick blanket of nurturing light, coating our skinny, filthy bodies. Inmates appeared at either side. One of them put their arm around my shoulder, another grabbed my hand. Then Jay started to speak.

"The path of the righteous man is beset on all sides by the iniquities of the selfish and the tyranny of evil men," he said, his tone slightly pitched and ragged. The line sounded familiar... He went on.

"Blessed is he, who in the name of charity and good will, shepherds the weak through the valley of darkness, for he is truly his brother's keeper and the finder of lost children." He walked around us then, sweeping his hands across the world below. His hands made grandiose spirals, his voice becoming louder and more forceful with every word.

"And I will strike down upon thee with great vengeance and furious anger those who would attempt to poison and destroy my brothers. And you will know my name is the Lord when I lay my vengeance upon thee!" The last part he yelled into the ether. Then he spun, a wicked grin hanging from his face.

We were all laughing. Delirious in the joy of simply being, we floated on a current of unburdened lightness. It was the briefest of moments, the shortest of breezes. Just a blip on the canvas of my life. But it was a moment that defined what I knew to be true: somewhere, out there, was the way out. It was all I'd ever needed to know.

The last days passed quickly. The forest took me in and bathed me in its glory. My hair was long. I shit in the woods and washed my face in streams. I wrote poems in time with the rhythm of streams, birds, and dripping water. Rain was a symphony that played against my tent; animals were messengers of grace and humility. I loved the end of the day, when I could take off my boots and walk barefoot through virgin soil. And then, we were in the van, heading back to civilization.

I was much more interested in saying goodbye to the other inmates than I was in greeting my mother, but that wasn't the case for them. I stood there awkwardly and waited next to my mother. I had no idea what to say. The awkwardness was relieved when the young woman inmate broke away, ran over, and wrapped me in a fierce hug. I knew that I would never see her again. The rules about that were strict and punishable by law. She was smiling, though, and that was enough for me.

The other inmates came over for their own hugs. These interactions were quick and tense, the emotional exchanges of men who have endured hardship together. We had been free in the wilderness to be ourselves. Now that we were back under the gazes of our families, we had adopted the coping strategies that had gotten us there. I pulled away from the last person and looked to my mother. I longed to be back on top of that mountain, far, far away.

The other families were still conversing and standing around when I turned, hefted my pack onto my shoulder, and went out the door. It was easy to spot the Jaguar parked in front. My mother grimaced when I threw my heavy backpack in through the rear door and muttered something about the leather. I climbed into the passenger seat, anxious and claustrophobic. After living in the forest for an extended period of time, it is an intense shock to suddenly come back to the world of pavement and advertisements. We never fully understand just how fast this world moves until we leave it. She quickly pulled out of the parking lot and rolled down the windows.

As we drove, she tried to stay conversational. She asked questions about 'my trip,' as if I had been lounging at the pool and playing dominoes. She rattled off details and data faster than I could comprehend. She had gone to Mexico while I'd been away. I had been fired from both of my jobs. My high school was threatening to expel me for not showing up on time. When my friends had called, wondering where I was, she had told them that I was at 'camp.' She had also read all of my journals and was offended by the things I had to say about her. Naturally, she had thrown them all away.

"You're lucky you're not headed to boarding school," she added.

We reached the beach house she had borrowed from a friend. The house was warm, familiar, and, most importantly, had a recently remodeled shower. Before the car had fully stopped, I was already rolling onto the driveway, headed to the back door I knew would be open. Within seconds, I had the water going, full blast and scalding hot.

Even the steam felt good. My oily, crusted clothes fell to the ground and stayed upright, resisting gravity. Thick socks peeled from my feet, pulling swatches of dead skin with them while releasing a colorful bouquet of aromas. I threw those directly in the trash. Then I threw open the door and walked into—

Heaven. Pure bliss. Angels sang and priceless gems fell from the sky in heaps. I felt as if there had been a parasitic crust on my skin, eating away at my soul like a snake eating its tail. The cascade of warm water and soap washed away all of the invading grime from my being. The floor of the shower ran dark red and brown, a combination of sweat, blood, sap, clay, sand, bark, and rich soil. It all flowed off of my body in a thick, choked stream.

Several rounds of lathering later, I sat down and let the water pound against my chest. When the water ran cold, I turned the nob then sat back down in the shower pan. I took my time cleaning and clipping my toe nails, shaving off the thick calluses, and spelunking in between my toes. The process was long. When I finished, I turned the water on and started the process all over again.

When I came out, my mother was sitting at the counter, a glass of wine in her hand. She smiled at me, the fake one she uses when she is trying to sell a house, and asked if I had left any hot water. I felt the contempt boil up into my chest. I could clearly see the self-obsessed, invidious person in front of me—incapable of looking at herself in the mirror; incapable of taking any kind of responsibility for her own actions; incapable of seeing anything aside from the slight inconvenience of having to wait an hour before she could take a shower herself.

I pushed my feelings down. That was the primary thing that I had learned. It wasn't okay to feel anger. In the presence of these people, it was a foolish mistake to feel anything at all.

Without meaning to, I had mastered an endurance-based, survival mentality. I looked at the snake in front of me. There would be no escape. I had to play the game for another two years. It was a lose-lose situation, a game I couldn't win, a game I was forced to play.

And in that moment, a new skill was born. I learned how to lie. I met her rheumy, unfocused eyes. I felt my shoulder blades creep backwards, my spine straightening. Then I smiled.

7

Soul Sister

> i will not last much longer
>
> here this memory is
>
> depreciative and dissociated
>
> i have to salvage
>
> a lasting peace

I had learned how to write poetry at 'camp.'

Like John Muir, my muse existed inside the mists of the deep forest at dawn, on the sides of unnamed ravines, and by the waning embers of the night's campfire. Since I had returned, I always kept a pad in my back pocket. The words were my release valve. My safety net. The pads were small enough to hide in the corners where she couldn't find them.

Things at school had taken a dramatic turn for the worse. I had returned as a pariah. Rumors about my trip to Myrtle Creek and my time at 'camp' had spread like wildfire. Everyone looked at me askance, as if I had an infectious disease. I had developed insomnia. Somehow I would appear at school each day, stumbling through the fluorescent lighting and bustling throngs, a walking zombie.

Eventually, I would wake up in one class or another. I was a social butterfly who didn't fit in anywhere. It felt like I was constantly dodging swiftly widening cracks in the floor. The small notebooks in my pocket seemed to be the only thing keeping me from falling through.

Somewhere along the line, my mother had discovered the wonders of pharmaceutical drugs. I have no idea which ones they were, but it was never long past dark that she would show up downstairs, ranting and raving about something we had done wrong. My brother was better at tuning her out than I was. I had to appease her. If she wasn't happy, then I wasn't safe. I would gently soothe her until she was done, then lead her back upstairs. Sometimes, I had to carry her. She didn't remember any of it the following day.

> with these blue roses and hydrangeas
>
> "light a candle." i whispered, chuckling
>
> "this hurts me more than it hurts you."
>
> i locked the door.

I started buying notebooks by the dozen.

They filled up quickly and formed piles underneath the loose floorboards of my room. Then I started buying marijuana. It made sense to me that someone who had attended drug rehabilitation should know a thing or two about drugs. It also was a great way to surround myself with other people. All I had to do was hold a lighter to a rolled-up joint and I was tacitly accepted into any group I wanted to be in. As long as my car had gas and I had a full bag, I wasn't alone anymore.

I honestly believed that constant anxiety was normal. I was a young adult, and that was just how life was. I knew that nowhere was safe and people will always betray you. Those things were obvious. Life was about gambling with your heart and your future as much as you could. Successful people were just the ones that hit with their bets. If I could just get lucky a few times, everything would be all right. Somewhere, somehow, I would finally feel whole. Somebody, something, would love me. It's not as if any of this meant anything, anyway.

> the neighbors across the street are watching
>
> a movie, the children curled up
>
> at the feet of the couch
>
> helpless blue halos hanging limp
>
> over their fallen heads.

I had been a rule follower my whole life. That was how to survive. If I could appease the monsters, I would make it long enough to get out of there.

All I had to do was tiptoe across the floors, keep up with the constantly changing expectations, and maintain the peace at all costs. But somewhere in the wilderness, the curtain had been drawn back to reveal... nothing. I'd seen how vulnerable I was. It was all a giant lie, a scam designed to keep me as a well-functioning sewer system for my housemates.

I had never stepped a foot out of line, yet they blamed me anyway. I figured, if I was going to be treated like a criminal, I might as well reap the benefits of being one. I started to rebel.

My first love was graffiti. I would creep out of my window late at night, cans rattling in my backpack, stopping frequently to smoke a joint in the woods. Between school, sports, and late-night adventures, I was never home. I would appear briefly, crawling through the same window I left from, around five o' clock. If she had returned home that night, I would make my presence known. An hour or so would pass before I could hear her coming down the stairs for a second bottle of wine. After she went upstairs, I was free.

> standing in the hall i feel a breeze
>
> but the windows are closed.
>
> the computer screen flashes no line
>
> over and over again. i open the door
>
> to the moon howling
>
> lonely without his old friend.
>
> cats are fighting in the alley.

A sense of doom had collected in the corners of my mind. Everything could crash down at any time. The marijuana soothed the anxiety, replacing it with numbness. And in the vacuous emptiness, the insidious roots of apathy grew like kudzu. I'd lost morality and direction. I was a rudderless ship adrift in a dead zone.

I still went to school. That was part of the charade. It was my junior year, but I already had enough credits to graduate. My high school had a program that would send you to the nearest university if they had classes you wanted to take that they didn't offer. I jumped at the opportunity. So, I was employed and a college student. But my eighteenth birthday was still a long way away. I still had to play the damn game.

One morning, as I trudged through the packed halls to my locker, I ran into an acquaintance holding a stack of papers. She quickly mentioned that she was taking a few of her poems to the school's annual publication, then scurried away. A voice from deep within whispered. Without thinking, I followed her to the library, where a poster was tacked to the wall outside.

It was a school-wide contest. And the submissions were anonymous! I left immediately and drove back to my mother's house. The next few hours were a frenzy. I wrenched apart notebooks, tearing poems out in clumps. I hurriedly copied them onto clean, white printer paper. Under each poem, I wrote the initials: S.S. With the high-pitched shrill of the day's last bell still ringing through the halls, I arrived at the office doors. They were just closing the submissions box. The teacher in charge sighed and reopened the lid. I stuffed the loose papers into the box, blew him a kiss, then darted out the door.

I'd forgotten about it when, two weeks later, I stood at my locker, staring at the exit door at the end of the hallway. Without warning, a group of theater kids, dressed up in fancy suits that easily cost more than my car, surrounded me. All of them were dancing and singing a show tune I couldn't recognize. Then, without further ado, the leader handed me a Burger King crown, decorated in puff paint. I had won, they said. And because of the anonymity required, they had taken my initials and given me a pseudonym: Soul Sister.

"Aren't you excited!?" one of them screamed.

But I couldn't hear. Emotions poked through the numb facade of my mask. First, there was a surge of pride, recognition, and validation. That disappeared just as fast as it arrived, replaced with a flash of rage, and followed by a torrential downpour of hopelessness. I was practicing what I had learned at 'camp.' Stuff it down. Put one foot in front of the other. Keep it cool until I can escape...

Soul Sister. My poems were my art. In those pages was a fledgling identity, born from the deepest and most vulnerable parts of myself. I had tentatively stepped out into the world, toeing the waters of purpose and hope. And these rich, entitled monsters had just spat it all back in my face. I wanted to break their noses, to rip their arms from their sockets... Instead, I stuffed it down.

I gave them a quiet thanks, then turned my back. I stood there, clutching the paper crown with both hands, well past when the bell rang. Then I slowly closed the locker, still empty, slung my backpack over my shoulder, and walked outside.

I almost ran right into the Vice Principal, who was kneeling just outside the door, rubbing some solvent on what looked to be a hastily drawn swastika. He was the one who had engineered my early release. Maybe he had seen my 'permanent record.' Or maybe he was just a good man.

"Picked up another shift?" He asked, flashing a knowing smile.

"Something like that." I replied. I didn't look at him. I knew that if I did, I would start to cry. I hurried to my car, drove to the park, and smoked a joint. Then I called the pizza place where I worked. They did need an extra hand, after all.

this is a foreign house on foreign soil

adrift on a greased hot-plate

there is no messiah for this *choza*

facing a trial by fire.

The next day, there was a school assembly. I hadn't been to one of them in years. It was child's play getting around the silly requirements. I would hand a nugget to one of the other kids in class, who would then fake bowel problems, go to the bathroom, and call me out of class. It was easy for anyone to pretend they were my father because no one had ever met him.

But that day was different. I'd come in late, having fallen asleep in the parking lot. There was no getting out of this one.

The students and faculty droned on for hours, praising this and that, doing their best to make it all sound relevant. I had dozed off somewhere along the way when I was rudely jabbed in the ribs. I startled awake, bleary-eyed, my glasses barely staying on my face. There were faces. Thousands of them. And a lot of them were staring right at me. Mostly because there was a guy in a kingly purple outfit, reaching toward me to hand me... another paper crown.

I took a quick glance at the cardboard headpiece. The writing was the same as the first. 'Soul Sister' was broadly emblazoned across the front. They were announcing the winners of the contest and asking them to put their crowns on and stand and... I crumpled mine up and tossed it into the seat next to me. My girlfriend was three rows below. She had her camera out, a smile plastered to her face, which rapidly disappeared when she saw mine. I stood.

The high school was a large one. There were easily three thousand kids in attendance, probably more, the narrow bleachers packed to the brim and groaning under the weight of so many bodies. I pushed through the throng. Several curses and threats followed. I could barely hear them. A ringing had started in my ears. My vision was narrow, blurring, with dots encroaching along the periphery. Stuff it! I could feel the eyes, smell the judgment... Stuff it-

Mercifully, I reached the doors before the security guard. The Vice Principal was there. He started to put up his hand, then slowly lowered it. I saw his eyes for the first time. Lined. Weathered. Kind. He must have seen something in mine as well.

"Picked up another shift?" he said, cracking the door open behind him. This time, I said nothing. I could feel the hardware melting underneath the hood, the engine overheating in the garage. I couldn't have spoken if I'd wanted to. I passed through the door like a rat squirming between two fence posts.

"I really liked that one about the house," he said to my back. "Pretty dark though!" I started jogging toward the door.

I felt a twinge in my chest as something very small and extremely delicate snapped in half. Over the past six months, everything I had known to be true had crumbled in my hand. Justice? Gone. My sense of righteousness? Scribbled on countless walls in bright spray paint. Integrity? Nope. And family values? Don't even get me started. As I crossed the threshold, out into the furiously pouring rain, I knew that the only thing I would ever have was the pad of paper in my back pocket. And all that seemed to bring was shame.

I picked up speed as I hit the parking lot. My clothes were soaked when I jumped in my car and peeled out. Time passed, but there was no one there to clock it. I was driving, I knew that much, and at some point, coffee and gas appeared in the car. Smoke curled across the windshield, the windows cracked, rain pounding down in an apocalyptic torrent of water and relief. Despite the conditions, I felt safe then. As long as the wheels were rolling, nothing could hurt me.

It was long past dark when I arrived at my mother's house. A letter was sitting on the kitchen table. It was open, of course, despite being addressed to me. I scanned it quickly as the sound of disjointed steps rumbled from upstairs. There was an event planned for the winners of the contest. A reading at Powell's, where we were expected to get up and read one of our winning entries.

"You entered a contest?" she asked incredulously.

"Yeah. I won," I said, still staring at the piece of paper. The event was the following Thursday. "I don't-"

"Where do I RSVP? I've got a date that night, but we can definitely..." I had already thrown the paper on the table and started heading toward the basement. Her words were slurred. I couldn't lie anymore. I heard her voice as I descended.

"...you shouldn't be so moody all the time..."

I stopped on the last stair, grit my teeth, and punched the air. Fifteen minutes later, I was backed up against the shower, cold water raging against the pane behind me. Moody? Moody?! I couldn't feel anything but pure, white, unadulterated hate. But that's not what 'good boys' feel. 'Good boys' are never angry. I lit up another joint and blew it up toward the exhaust fan. Stuff it.

I'll show you moody...

an oppressive stench pierces my nostrils

and quickly my tattered jeans are spattered.

from deep within a trance

i emerge

docile as ever.

I walked into Powell's on Thursday, a light drizzle slicking the pavement on Burnside. My girlfriend tried to hold my hand, but I missed the gesture. She had been looking at me funny all day, as if I was keeping a secret from her. I couldn't focus on that. The only thing I could think about was getting it over with.

The irony of this was that Powell's was my happy place. A massive, sprawling bookstore, a literary behemoth planted smack dab in the center of Portland. It was always bustling. I loved to get lost in the aisles, coffee in hand, brushing the titles with two fingers as I passed by. The smell alone left me enchanted.

A few times, I had been stopped by security on the way out and searched. I didn't blame them. Between my hi-tops, ragged jeans, and long, shaggy hair, I didn't look like I was there to do anything but steal. After the third time it happened, I looked the man dead in the eye and held up my hands.

"I just don't have anywhere else I want to be," I told him. They left me alone after that.

The same man nodded to me as we walked in. We passed through the familiar aisles, cutting across the colors until we reached the administrative side of the building. The comforting aromas followed us up as we took the stairs two at a time. Public speaking had always mortified me. But that wasn't the source of my terror. My feet began to tremble as we neared the top.

Luckily, I was first. I was the 'most published,' with five or six entries accepted. My girlfriend also knew a bunch of the theater kids who had worked on the publication. She had pulled a few strings.

There was close to a hundred people cramming the wide meeting hall. I could see my mother and her date, chattering away in the back. A few of the teachers gave short speeches, then one called my name. I didn't hear it. I was looking around, hoping the power would go out... My girlfriend sharply elbowed me in the ribcage and I jolted back to reality. Then toward the audience. Every single pair of eyes was resolutely fixated on me.

Showtime!

I didn't bother with an introduction. I pulled open one of the books, found the right poem, and started reading. I could feel the tension and unease as everyone comprehended what I was reading, and to whom. When I was finished, I was almost breathless. The weight of a thousand steel beams was pushing my shoulders into a pronounced sag. Before I uttered the last words, I was already crumpling the pages between my hands.

> Suddenly the night is warm and bright
>
> disrupted only by the distant wail of sirens
>
> and the flapping of sandals, swiftly pounding
>
> on the cracked pavement.

I tossed the book toward the front row and walked out. I could hear halting, confused clapping. I found out later that I was supposed to say some words, read a few pieces, and then, introduce the next person. Either no one had told me or I'd missed the relevant details. I was halfway down the stairs before I heard someone coming after me. It didn't matter who it was. All that mattered was getting out of there.

My breath caught and halted. I was a wide-eyed soldier staggering away from the battlefield. I slammed into the heavyset metal door and exploded out into the alleyway. The MAX was going by, its dull, muted bell chiming as it ushered along a burst of warm city air. I could hear my girlfriend calling behind me.

I couldn't think. I could barely see. I had stuffed it all so deep that I couldn't feel it anymore. My invisible hand reached deep, trying to draw something out, but there was nothing to hold. I was an empty vessel, left to collect whatever the sky thought I was worthy of. At the moment, that seemed like precious little.

I started to run.

8

Road Rash

The wind whipped through my hair as I dodged annoyed students on the narrow path. We rode along the main artery between the college and the stadium, behind which were the apartments reserved for students. I rode a borrowed racing bike. It was amazingly light, picked up speed effortlessly, and had a middle finger sticker superglued over the back reflector. It was more than a bike. I was flying.

College had been an even mix of reckless partying and a rampantly irresponsible workload. My parents had somehow squandered the college money that had been left to me by my dead grandparents. I had found out that the funding had been cut during my first semester. This had led to some hard thinking. Ultimately, I had decided to power through, taking double the regular amount of classes at once and working three jobs to pay it. Whenever I could, I got wasted.

Miraculously, I had made some friends along the way. Whenever I wasn't working, studying, or half-assing my extra online classes, I was sitting on a ledge somewhere, passing a blunt and a 40. We listened to a lot of Bay Area hip hop and talked about philosophy. We had secret handshakes and code words. We had all gotten a house together after the first year, a massive building that was perfect for keggers.

One day, a woman had fallen through the laundry chute while I was taking a shower. With shampoo pouring over my tangled mess of hair, I had jumped out to help her up...

"Just wanted to know what I was working with ahead of time," she said, stifling a grin. I stared dumbly. Then she giggled and fled from the room. By the time I got out of the shower, I was in love.

It was the first time most of us had lived on our own, and we were taking full advantage of our freedom. We had more bongs than sense and our stereo system was the bane of the neighborhood. A steady stream of visitors appeared, coming and going like tufts of smoke. We lived on the sand, forever ready for a game of beer pong or a cigarette.

Somewhere along the line, we had all realized that we were getting lazy and out of shape. So we had started going to the gym together. We were riding back home from one of these sessions.

My roommates were way behind me. Mack was the gym rat among us. He was short but stout, with curly hair that bloomed in all directions like a hydrangea bush. George was like me, skinny and tall, with the calmly resolute face of someone determined to find a better life. We were all ready to grow, physically and mentally, in the radiating heat of the Willamette Valley sun. I felt invincible, which explained why I was shirtless and didn't have a helmet. For some reason, I decided to start a race. I was winning with ease. When I looked back, there was no one behind me.

A split second later, I turned my head forward and registered the turn ahead. It was a nasty one, more than ninety degrees, and lined with thick blackberry bushes on both sides. There was no time to react. I hit the brakes and managed to straddle just enough of the rocky outcrop of the edge of the path to stay upright. Time slowed as the razor thin tires of the bike balanced on the knife's edge of concrete. This was a delicate dance, a harrowing negotiation. A brief flicker of hope danced across my mind—then I hit a small divot and my body was airborne.

There is always a moment when you are flying through the air when you realize that you've fucked up. Where you can do nothing but hope that you are going to live through it. Inevitably your instincts and will to live kick in. In my case this was raising one arm across my face and the other toward the ground in a desperate attempt to mitigate the damage. A thought crossed my mind.

This is going to hurt.

I took the first impact on my left rib cage. I could feel at least one of them snap. Then my momentum lifted my legs all the way up in the air, ruthlessly slamming my body back down onto the pavement. I was sliding like steel wool across an unfinished cutting board coated with cheese.

It wasn't over. Inertia kept me tumbling, this time into thorns of thick bramble. I could feel my sundered skin. I could sense the ruptured bones. My body swelled. I could identify every one of the wicked thorns lancing me in innumerable places. I tried to gasp, tried to cry, tried to make any sound at all, but couldn't. I nestled into the relative comfort of the blackberry bushes and thorns. I could taste blood. Dimly, I heard a woman screaming in the distance.

I must have passed out, because the next thing I remember is being forcefully dragged out of the bushes. As the two sets of arms heaved, I felt a cascade of pops down my right side. It was the cartilage of my ribcage tearing and detaching. When I was clear of the bramble's clutches, I fell to my knees and heaved. The puddle in front of me was dark and viscous. All blood. My head was swimming. I looked to my left and saw my buddies. Somehow, words came out.

"This *hurts*, Mack," I rasped. Each word felt like it was pulled, naked, ass-backward, and screaming, through a cornfield. My legs shook as I started to walk. Hands appeared, trying to hold me back. I shoved them away. I wasn't going to be carried out of there, and I needed to get home before the adrenaline wore off. The path seemed unreasonably long ahead.

"Someone get me a ride.," I said over my shoulder.

I reached a break in the trees. The sun shone dimmer now, a haze coating my retinas and making everything appear rosy red. The pain was everywhere, everything. It was hilarious. I remembered the night in Southern Oregon… I was in shock. Mack rode by, guiding my bike alongside with his right hand.

"I've got painkillers at the house!" He yelled back. Then he was gone.

George came from behind me and tried to help me walk. I simply pointed to my ribcage.

"Broken." I said, grimacing. He nodded and shook his head. He was a stoic, that one.

Then we heard footsteps. It wasn't unusual for such a busy path. But this was different. We lived in Track Town, USA. There were runner's clubs, cross-country teams, Club Running Adventures, and, of course, the National Champion Track Team. It was the latter that was coming down the path. Hundreds of lithe, beautiful women, covered in glistening spandex, bouncing and bobbing their way forward. Each one radiated an aura of health and vitality, a pure white transcendence that…

I looked down. Gashes and bruises covered my body. Blood seeped from dozens of wounds. I could feel dripping on both of my pinkies, seeping down along the asphalt embedded in my elbows and forearms. It didn't take long for them to reach us. We were in the middle of the path. I couldn't deviate, so straight ahead we went. The waves of women separated before me, every eye glued to my nearly naked, serrated skin. I caught eyes with one and winked at her. She suddenly looked nauseous.

A horn brayed, and the women started to run faster. I looked up and behind the throng was a rusting, cherry-red Ford Explorer. I knew that car. I had spent long hours in the passenger seat, getting high and listening to Dubstep. That would be Cutty, one year older than us, and my best friend on campus. He also, conveniently for me, lived nearby. That glorious, indestructible chariot was blazing down the narrow asphalt, horn blaring, with Cutty's giant head hanging out the window.

"QUIT GRAB-ASSING AND GET YOUR ASS IN THE CAR!!" he bellowed.

I got to the door, and several hands hauled me into the front seat. There were towels down to catch the blood. Cutty thrust a loaded pipe in my hands, then slammed the car into reverse. He drove as if possessed, skidding around turns and bouncing over speed bumps. We were at my house in minutes. I tried not to look at the blankets I had ruined. The car shook and shimmied as he drove across the overgrown lawn, then came to a sliding stop. Cutty didn't ask my opinion. He threw open my door, thrust his arms underneath my back and legs, and carried me inside.

More roommates appeared, each with their own blend of curiosity, pity, and horror glued to their faces. When I got to the kitchen there were shot glasses, a bottle of liquid hydrocodone, and a larger bottle of vodka. I raised the liquor bottle and chugged, then chased it with several shots of painkiller. Nothing happened. I began to set up another round, but someone held my hand.

A half dozen sets of eyes stared at my body. We all knew what came next. I had to shower. You could see the road rash; the thick swathes of pavement tattooed onto my skin. Some of the wounds had already caked, while some continued to ooze. It all had to be cleaned. Immediately.

The sound of a door slamming reached us from the other room, and my laundry chute princess sprinted in. I didn't remember calling her. There was no time to think about it. When she saw the road rash and blood, she gasped and started cooing in my ear. Her hands fluttered and probed, looking for a way to grab hold. I winced and shuddered at the faintest breeze. She gave up being gentle, firmly wrapped a hand around my waist, and led me down the hallway.

We hobbled to the shower, where she helped me undress. I knew that I was going to be laid up for a very long time. I would lose my jobs, miss countless classes, and most likely run out of money. I had raced ahead at breakneck speed for so long that the fear of having to slow down was worse than anything. I quickly found myself in an all-new kind of shock.

With a groaning of old pipes and the hiss of cold water, the water hit the pan. Pain began to seep through my brain's protective layers. Endless waves of agony seared across my body. Hundreds of aches and pains all clamored for attention, a chorus of voices that screamed in a symphony of brutality, each one begging for dominance. I turned to her then.

As more clothes came off, her face was turning paler. It became translucent, gaunt, and was holding faraway eyes in a desperate clutch. In a flash, I was back in that garage, watching Aaron nervously gutting fish in the sink. I could feel the grip of that walkie-talkie phone in my hand... I snapped back into my battered body and stepped into her. She trembled at the touch, then fell deep into my chest.

"It's so bad... so bad..." she started. Her voice tapered off into a high squeak. I could feel her tears rolling down to my belly button.

I cut her off. "Want to order pizza and get drunk tonight?" I asked. Always had a way with the ladies, this guy. A real Don Juan, a soothsayer. She nodded, though. More tears crept down my chest.

A loud knock ended the moment. Steam had filled the room, pouring outward as someone handed her a stack of washcloths and a sponge through a crack in the door. As she began to close it, the door reopened and the bottle of vodka was thrust through as well. What are friends for?

She stepped to the shower, opened the door, and pressed the bottle firmly into my hand. I took a long, resigned breath. I felt the heat in my spine. I felt the ache in my soul.

This is going to hurt.

9

PATSY

I'd caught the wrong bus and ended up on the far end of town. The wheel underneath my seat continued to churn, spraying water in all directions. A massive engine roared behind me, also churning... Come to think of it, everything was churning. The rain outside the window... my guts... my heart...

I looked up and saw another strip club pass. Bright lights in pastel colors lit up the shoddy paint and rotting boards. I knew where I was. I didn't remember switching buses. I had 'pre-gamed' at my house, drinking and smoking everything I had available to get ready for what I was timidly assuming was a date with my coworker.

So this was adulthood, eh?

I'd graduated college a year early, filled with the grim determination that only a failing economy can give you. After months of resumes, cover letters, interviews, and long days in the coffee shop, I reached the conclusion that I needed to take any job that would have me. I walked from door to door, handing resumes to people who would no doubt throw them away as soon as my back was turned. I wore a button-up shirt, slacks, and a tie. I was desperate.

I saw her as soon as I walked through the door of the sandwich shop. She looked up from counting her tips with the most beautiful expression

I'd ever seen. There is no point in describing it. Every man knows that expression. I stopped, stunned, completely speechless as the door came back and hit me in the ass. I moved toward the counter and asked her if they were hiring, hoping that I sounded confident. She smirked at that. Oh, joy of joys! Oh sweet, rapturous tendrils of heaven! Her smile stoked the once-doused flame of my heart. It roared to a brief crescendo, a match head destined to burn, burn, bu—

"Hellooooo...?"

She was looking. Right at me. She was looking right at me. Right.

I thrust out my resume. This time she laughed. I tried to breathe. I'd forgotten my own name. I would have been hard-pressed to identify which planet I was on. She said something.

Luckily, she also pointed to the left. When I was able to tear my head away, an older, shrew-like blonde woman was standing there, also grinning. Her smile was vicious, though. The kind you see before the trap door opens. She enthusiastically shook my outstretched hand with both of hers, then gestured to a table where we could sit down and talk.

Before the day was over, I was the new kitchen manager. It was my show, seven days a week. The restaurant became my life. It was a grease-soaked cell, but it got me my own apartment. The chains were strong and heavy. The job quickly wore me down—mentally, physically, and emotionally. What kept me there was the view out of the small service window.

There is nothing quite like the relationship between a cook and a waitress. It is a mixture of mutual parasitism and symbiosis. The cook has to do the dirty work, sweating and burning, scraping and cleaning, so that the food can appear. The waitress has to buffer the cook from the outside world. It should come as no surprise that both types of people are heavily tattooed, jaded, and world-weary, and that they frequently fall in love with each other.

She would make sure to stand with her back to the window whenever she could, framing herself in the open door beyond. Sunlight would cascade across her flyaway hair, silhouetting her slim shoulders and tight-fitting overalls that didn't hide a thing... She would always feel me staring, my jaw forever reaching, straining to get to the floor. She would turn and flash the same grin. Sometimes, she would even come to the window, press her arms up against the sides of the narrow opening, and reach in as if to hold my hand...

Months passed like this. We began to go on dates. At least, I thought they were dates. I was nervous, too jittery to do more than laugh and light cigarettes. I let her do all the talking, listening intently as she rattled off factoids and idiosyncrasies. I repeatedly got lost in the lines of her face, the deep hazel of her eyes, or the slight curve of...

By night, I was a music writer. This was right at the advent of online publications. My editor would pass me a list of shows in the area, and I would pick a handful, usually unknown bands that could use the publicity. The shows were always the same: dingy dive bars with cheap booze, mediocre sound systems, and a thick haze of smoke drifting across walls that hadn't been cleaned in decades.

I was introduced to a large number of women in The Scene. Occasionally, one of them would sidle up next to me during a set, tugging my arm away from my soggy notepad, and pull me to some dark corner. But that was just biding time. My thoughts were forever back in that kitchen; my heart draped on the clothesline hanging in that narrow service window.

In short, I was fucked. I had unwillingly gotten myself into the trap that so many men fall into: too timid to take the chance and yet too courageous to let it go. I wanted to believe that it was because I couldn't risk my job. Really, I just couldn't fathom the possibility that a woman like her could possibly want someone like me. There was no self-pity or despair. Instead, it was just a grim reality. I was an ugly, acne-riddled failure. A cook with a fancy degree. A waste of breath.

I walked her home every day. It happened naturally when we found out that I lived right next to her usual train stop. I would walk slow on purpose, drawing it out as we laughed and joked. We always arrived with her holding my arm, leaning into me as we passed the crazy folk on the sidewalk. Every day I tried to work up the nerve…

We shared a mutual love for the Portland Trail Blazers. One day, in the middle of the lunch rush, she hollered back that she had tickets to the game that night. My heart lurched, then imploded, then threw itself against the wall. I croaked out a cry of excitement. Without wondering where the tickets had come from, I loudly accepted. My jaw set. This was my chance. I was going to make 'the move.'

Now, there I was, gripping the front of the filthy bus seat, counting traffic lights. The anxiety was building toward a wild crescendo. I had gotten tight, overmedicated, and now the chance was slipping through my fingers. Time began to pass too rapidly, breaking off in chunks from the grand ice shelf of The Future. I was standing now, urging the bus to go faster, *faster*… I smashed the button and got off at the wrong stop, fifteen blocks away from her apartment, then broke into a run.

She opened the door, and the anger swept off of her face. I was coated in sweat and puffing heavily. She cracked a joke and beckoned me in. The first moments were painfully awkward. I didn't know whether to sweep her off her feet or find a place to sit. I did neither, standing there awkwardly until she wrapped me in a warm hug. My mind was in overdrive. I'd already blown it.

I should have...

She sensed my unease and went to her fridge, coming back with a beer that she thrust into my hand. I downed it quickly as she took a few shots. The apartment was close to the stadium, so if we hurried we could make it by the second quarter. I grabbed the bottle and helped myself. She stood close, but not touching.

Three or four shots later, we tottered to the street. My hands, forever in my pockets, were sweating as she slipped her arm through mine. Time blurred.

I came to sitting in the stadium. They were damn good seats. Definitely better than I could afford. I was no waitress, after all. She was grinning from ear to ear, a beer in one hand and a massive tub of popcorn in the other. Then I discovered, to my delight, that there was also a beer in *my* hand. I raised it triumphantly and toasted her. This was going to work out, after all.

At halftime, she disappeared for a while. I sat back and took in the stadium. The Rose Garden had always been my happy place. I loved the lights and sounds of the game; the roars of the crowd; all a blissful reprieve from the ever-pouring rain outside. The city loved this team. We were die-hards, fanatical observers of The Game in all of its glory.

Surrounding me was a cross section of the city's denizens: an older hippy couple with tie-dyed Grateful Dead t-shirts, a gaggle of young kids, bookended by chaperones on either side, groups of men—three to four abreast—knocking down beers and bellowing out all of the pent-up frustrations of the week. It was the beauty of chaos perfectly encapsulated in a well-lit bowl of humanity.

When she returned, she had an odd look on her face and a flower in one hand. It made me queasy, that slimy feeling that comes when something is just a little off but you can't figure out what it is. I tried to push it away. She was beautiful. Of course someone would hand her a flower. She sat down and we started trading jokes again. Soon enough, the game resumed and the intensity built throughout the stadium. Everyone was yelling and high-fiving. She clutched the massive container of popcorn like a young child would a teddy bear.

I sat down briefly to catch my breath and take a swig out of my beer. And then, out of nowhere, my favorite player swiped a steal, flew down the court, and let loose one of the biggest rim-rocking dunks I have ever seen. In one motion, I jumped up, throwing both of my arms into the air and... caught the greasy tub squarely on the bottom.

Popcorn flew into the air in a giant plume of buttered kernels, spreading out across the entire section. It coated dozens of people beneath us, all of whom looked up to stare at who had thrown it. I could feel my face burning. But I wasn't looking at them.

She was laughing, glee covering her face better than any makeup ever could. I melted like a marshmallow in the microwave. She put her hand on my arm, and the warmth of it passed across my entire body. It was what rapture felt like. Spiteful eyes bored into me from all directions, but I ignored them.

It was my moment. I pushed down the rising embarrassment, grinned, and leaned in for the kiss. I could feel the entire universe slowing down for this canon event. The music swelled toward a crescendo, the camera zoomed in from all angles, the crowd roared...

And she pulled away.

I quickly sat down and finished my beer. She made a joke about the game. Luckily, the intensity of the game picked up. Shame plastered my face and radiated to my cheeks, but it was passed off as enthusiasm. As soon as the horn sounded for the end of the third quarter, I hustled down to the snack shack to get another round. I was behind two guys dressed in jerseys and fitted hats. I could hear them over the sounds of the bustling crowd.

"Yeah, she got some tickets in the next section. She's with some guy…"

"Some GUY? She playing games, bro?"

"Yeah, she loves that shit. Said she's coming over later though…"

The shame hit then—a flood of it that threatened to sweep me out into the waiting gutters outside. I was shook, rattled to my bones. I was just the *patsy*. A tool she was using to get back at another guy. And I was *buying the beer*. The worst part was, this didn't stop me for a moment. I was caught in inertia, blindly following, meandering my way toward what I thought life was supposed to look like. I was lost and on the wrong bus. Again.

And there was still another quarter to go.

When I got back, I handed her a beer and surreptitiously glanced around. It didn't take long to spot them, on the same row, in the section to our right. They were staring right at me.

It felt like the world was crumbling beneath my feet, and the rumbling crowd would soon break loose the foundation of the world. I was teetering on the edge. She was fine though—laughing and hollering at every play. She took a swig and looked deeply into my eyes.

"Isn't this *great*?!"

When the game finally ended, I took my time getting up. I had to keep it together. I had to stuff it, deep down, until I could escape. I looked around the section. Popcorn was scattered across all of the seats. She accidentally clipped one of the beer bottles as she rose, and it fell, clanking down the cement stairs. We hustled away. At the top of the ramp, she tugged at my arm.

"I've got to go meet someone," she said, keeping her eyes forward.

"Okay. I'll see you tomorrow."

"Yeah."

I was a patsy. A pawn used as a shield. I beelined for the escalators. As I descended, I caught sight of myself in the massive windows. I didn't know the man I was looking at. As the crowds began to disperse ahead, I slipped out of the arena and lit a cigarette.

A massive line had formed at the MAX station. I lived thirty blocks away, but I knew I wouldn't be able to keep any of it down that long. I couldn't let anyone see me. The rain picked up as I made my way across the bridge. By the time I reached my apartment, I was soaked to the bone. Two of my neighbors were outside, huddled underneath a low overhang, sharing a joint.

"How was the game?" one of them asked.

"I lost."

10

Andy's Van

The van creaked and groaned underneath our feet. We were packed tightly along the bench seats, thirteen of us, jostling and swaying together as we sped down the winding mountain roads. With each banked turn, the girl next to me pressed into my side. After a while, she reached down into the cooler at our feet, grabbed a beer, and handed it to me. The can was still dripping ice, the mountains a bright blue in the lights of the passing cars. She turned her face up to me and smiled.

"Think you can double fist?" she asked, brightly.

I slipped my arm around her waist. Electricity surged through my hands and up my spine. She was soft, warm, and bite-sized. I could feel the strings under my heart being pulled... I let loose a wild yell, which was answered, in chorus, by the rest of the passengers. Andy cracked a grin and threw his shoulders back. He was offered several beers that he waved off. The aging VW didn't have power steering. His forearms bulged with the effort of steering down the banked turns.

I held her close, doing my best to shelter her from the press of sweat and elbows. A threadbare curtain leisurely slapped the back of my head. Music appeared from a portable speaker. Crooning country songs. We sang along, beers swinging freely, a chorus of off-key voices. I'd finally found it. Freedom.

***

After our last 'date,' I tried to keep it together, but the illusion had been shattered. The walls of the kitchen had begun to compress, creeping closer and closer by the minute. I threw myself at the work, ignoring the window, staring resolutely at the knife in my hands. Food got made.

I told my editor that I wanted more responsibility. Every night was a different venue, hundreds of sweating, swirling bodies jostling the ever-present beer in my hand. I would stay halfway through the set and write my story on the bus ride home. My alarm was set for four a.m. the next day.

The seams had begun to fray. I found myself dozing off while standing. It was unsustainable. Something had intervened. The kitchen job crumbled. The owner sent out an email, saying that the business had folded, and that there was no reason to show up the next day. Our checks would be sent via mail.

After a day of self-pity, I got back to the job board. A flash of inspiration, unconnected to anything I had been pursuing, led me to a job board solely for positions in the National Parks. The ad for bussers on Mt. Rainier clicked itself. Information scrolled across the screen, a self-filling application half-hidden with cigarette smoke. An hour later, my phone rang. Two weeks after that, I was on the train, heading north.

***

Andy had been the first person to take an interest in me. There were others, of course. It was an uncommonly well-matched cast of characters. Everyone got along well, the overall demeanor intensely positive. Our days were spent serving highly-processed food to tourists. Our nights were spent outside, bodies spread in the middle of the prodigious flower fields, crushed cans the only evidence of our passing through Paradise.

Andy had taken me under his wing, although I didn't understand that then. He invited me on activities that had nothing to do with the ongoing party. I found myself sitting shotgun in the van, cigars carefully tilted out of the windows, a flask rocking back and forth in the front cup holder. He taught me how to look people in the eye, stand up straight, and keep my cool in the workplace. His van quickly became a symbol for everything I hoped to be one day.

I'd told him about the girl. How she made my hands sweat when she looked at me. How she would draw hearts on my beer cans with a Sharpie. How I was starting to feel about her... He had initially counseled caution, but quickly changed tactics. We came up with masterful schemes. Midnight picnics in the flower fields. Improvised locks in the laundry room. And now, a 'spur-of-the-moment' dash down to Ashford for karaoke night. She loved karaoke. And I can sing. We figured ourselves to be evil geniuses. Villains with hearts of gold.

We weren't completely childish. Someone always called the bar ahead of our arrival. It was just the polite thing to do, considering Andy's van wasn't the only vehicle in our parade and our arrival instantly doubled the town's population. We would routinely show up, buy up all of the beer at the local market, then totter across the street to the lone bar—a drunken horde, ready to let loose.

We were typically met with a mixture of scorn from the locals and enthusiastic smiles from the bartenders. That night, the lights had already been dimmed. An older man stood in the corner, doing his best to massacre a Garth Brooks song. Rusted street signs lined the walls, reflecting the words dripping their way down the screen. I went to the bar and ordered two beers. When I handed one to the girl, she popped the tab, put up her index finger, then chugged it in one try. With a hearty swing, she then slammed it on the table in front of her. A belch roared from her abdomen, shaking her entire frame.

Her eyes were trained directly on me. Unwavering. "Wanna dance, handsome?" She said. An aftershock burp tumbled out.

Perfection.

I took her by the waist and led her to the middle of the dance floor. She grabbed my hand, leapt backward, and threw her arm wide behind her. I caught a bald head out of the corner of my eye. I turned to see Andy at the bar, chatting up the youngest of the bartenders. He was staring in my direction and flashed a wink. I felt an insistent tugging on my arm and turned back around.

The girl was sliding across the cracked wooden parquet floor, her blue dress turned into a rainbow by the multi-colored lights coming from the ceiling. Her grin was bright and purple. I could feel the eyes on us. The boys had been rooting for me for weeks now. I could almost see Andy's hand, raised up for a high five…

Good plan, good sir.

The ride up the mountain was smoother than the way down. I had taken the front passenger seat. The girl sat in my lap, double-fisting. After every turn, she would hold one of the cans to my lips, invariably missing the mark and streaking the front of my sweat-soaked shirt with warm beer. The young bartender straddled the cooler behind, leaning forward to talk to Andy as we rose up the mountain.

Periodically, we would stop, the entire caravan following our lead, and pile out into the cold mountain air. Mortars and bottle rockets appeared from nowhere, shooting off in brilliant displays across the virgin wilderness. Greens, purples, reds, and yellows erupted in the sky.

I cast cursory glances up at them, far more interested in how they lit up the upturned face next to me. We carried on this way up the entire road. On the last pullout, before we got within view of the Ranger Station, we stopped again. The last of the mortars hit the sky with a *whomp*. This time they were all white, showering down in brilliant, fire-ensconced pearls.

I couldn't wait anymore. I stepped in front of her and lowered my head... I was too drunk though. I didn't make it all of the way. I was caught in no man's land, not sure of where my head was, not wanting to head-butt her—she saved me by grabbing the front of my shirt and rudely pulling me to her face.

Our teeth clicked, our tongues met. Time stopped completely. The fireworks had dissipated shortly before, but another flash cracked across the pitch blackness. I opened my eyes to see one of the other girls holding a camera and smiling. I grabbed her hand and we piled back in the van.

Up the hill we went, singing and swaying. No cars passed us on the narrow highway. It was just us and the thick wooded—Suddenly, the high beams caught a massive shape in the middle of the road. Thickly bound legs pressed into the cracked pavement, four of them, pulsing and churning. The beast was massive and gleaming. A bright white tail, bushy and short, went straight upwards, defying gravity. It roared up the road ahead. Keeping pace. *Setting* the pace.

The silence in the van was impressive, if only for the juxtaposition from a few moments before. Every jaw sat, firmly planted, on the van floor. What use are words when you are witness to a miracle? What do you say when you are in the presence of a mythical beast? Of God itself?

The stag ran. Upwards it climbed, tirelessly galloping, its hooves a bright blur against the stark realities beneath. Andy kept the van at a healthy distance, just close enough to view but far enough not to threaten.

We went on this way for miles—endless minutes caught in the spinning, double helix of the universe. We were nothing, just entities paying for our existence with our attention. The girl grabbed my hand tightly, hard enough that I could feel her through the trance. This wasn't just any stag. This was *the stag*. A creature of legend. An omen from the Creator. Our paltry homage in the form of childish love and store-bought fireworks must have tickled the fancy of beings above our paygrade.

With a swift kick, it darted away from the highway. Thick bundles of muscle shone in the sharp head lights, defining bristling haunches. Clumps of dirt flew into the air behind him. Then it was gone.

Silence reigned. The entire van was stricken. Dumbfounded.

"What the hell *was* that?" someone asked. Everyone laughed. Andy looked at me, winked, then floored the accelerator. The bartender reached over and grabbed his arm. The girl on my lap lifted the beer to my lips. This time, most of it made it into my mouth. I squeezed her side, her thigh, her hand. I held on for dear life as beer dribbled down the side of my face. A hiccup tore from my chest and she giggled. It was a good question though.

What the hell was that?

11

THE HIGH ROAD

The Girl had cheated on me while I was at a funeral. I'd returned to Utah to find her holding some boy's hand, dull eyes staring through me without recognition. A man named Shane saved me from myself. He'd galloped down the hill, bushy mustache bobbing, cowboy boots spitting red dirt in all directions.

Evidently, I'd punched the new boyfriend in the face. I had no recollection of that. I spent a week on Shane's property in Tropic, spitting at snakes, one hand on a bottomless bottle of Jack Daniels, the other on a Marlboro. We were proper cowboys, the two of us. It was there that I learned how to scream.

The next four months were slow torture. I ran back to Portland as soon as I could. Then there were two more funerals in rapid succession. My mother was a mess. I still thought that I had to save her. I still believed that I could save anyone.

I picked up a job at a pot farm just outside of town, trimming buds and dragging massive plants around. A catatonic malaise pushed deeper on my lungs with each passing hour. My days off were spent at the bar. I picked fights, spat into empty bottles, and incinerated every bridge I walked across. It didn't take long before I burned the relationships with my childhood pals. My best friend left a bag of old stuff on my mother's porch. We never spoke again after that.

The pot farmers got sick of my attitude and threw me out, so I went back to the well. Lies and a fake mask of positivity got me a job as a waiter at Sol Duc Hot Springs. It was a small resort, tucked away in the middle of Olympic National Park, a dark corner just far enough away from Oregon to properly hide in. Water fell from the sky constantly, more persistent than insistent, a blanket of mist that occasionally upped its efforts. It is a rain forest, after all.

The windows of the restaurant looked out toward the pools. They were still blue in the morning, before the accumulated sweat and grime turned the water a sickly shade of green. I loved to watch the steam rising, thin tendrils fondly reaching out to the soft, perpetual massage of water coming from above. It was a marriage of sorts. One destined to last. Steam also rose from my mug of coffee, a subtle nod to the parallels between our brief, evanescent existences and the immutable processes of nature...

I had quickly found that philosophizing was the best way to escape the physical limitations of the restaurant I was clocked into.

I worked split shifts. This is a special kind of hell reserved for only the most wretched of service industry laborers. I fit the description well. Everything I owned fit in a small rucksack, and there was nothing to go back to.

When I'd been offered the job during the initial interview, I'd managed to play it cool for a few minutes. Then, I'd asked how soon I could start. Now that I was working from four in the morning to eleven at night, with no days off, my previous enthusiasm seemed... outdated.

The battle to stay sane was constant. There was no internet, cable television, or transportation available for the employees. I had gotten drunk at some point and made myself Public Enemy No. 1. The toxicity crept in from all directions, cutting the hopes of a renewed sense of community at the base of the trunk. I responded by receding inwards. Each day saw me becoming angrier and more temperamental. By the end of the third week, I felt close to the breaking point. And the season had barely begun.

Rain continued to fall and the tension continued to rise. There was simply no space to hide from one another. We all lived upstairs in the lodge, four to eight people to each bunk room, with a small dining/recreation room at the end of the hall. A nightly poker game was the negotiating table; international waters patrolled by each respective nation state. Taking each other's money was the only way we knew to transmute the reciprocal passive aggression.

My self-esteem was at an all-time low. In order to love myself, everyone else had to love me first. People who didn't like me became a challenge, a game that I had to win. The rampant liquor intake was just the necessary fuel for these ill-conceived attempts to bridge the divide.

As had become a trend in my life, a mentor appeared. The one's name was Brian. He was an ex-con, covered in tattoos, with chipped front teeth and broad shoulders. We bonded over a similar sense of humor and a deep, passionate love of scotch. He knew what it was like to be the odd man out.

I could tell he had taken me under his wing when he stopped stealing nips of my flask and got his own. We would sit for hours by the side of the river a short walk away, tossing rocks into the swift current and talking about life. He would give me pointers on how to blend in and be less obstinate. I know now that he was teaching me to 'mask' as well as he knew how. It was a survival technique one learns either in captivity or in a life lived in loneliness. What he didn't realize was that I was already an expert at it. This was just a place that didn't accept my mask.

It didn't take long for me to go completely haywire. I stopped sleeping entirely. Days would pass and I would hardly notice. I was a walking zombie, darting from table to table, then up the stairs to my bunk. I knew that I needed to get out of there. Luckily, the checks were good and there was nowhere to spend them, which meant I had quickly saved up enough to buy a car. Not a nice car. Definitely not one of those. But a vehicle, nonetheless. A ticket away from what had become a dreary, soul-sucking slog. Finding one quickly became an obsession.

The tumultuous events of the past few months had shocked me to the core. My inner temple had been breached. And if Brian taught me anything, it was to never, ever let the world into your private sanctum. Our entire culture and society are now built upon the vilification of men, simply for existing. If a man entertains even the vague notion that this is somehow correct... well. I had done exactly that.

What had once been an air-tight haven, protected from one and all, was now a raging battlefield. I couldn't stuff it anymore. I was dying of thirst in a rain forest, a sieve held up to the sky in a pathetic attempt to catch the falling drops. And my anger and frustration were only adding more holes to the bowl.

It was a Thursday, just after dinner, and a small group of us were walking along the path away from the lodge. The river was loud and boisterous, perfect for drowning mental machinations and overloaded processors. The night was just like any other. The rain drizzled. Steam rose. The smell of sulfur permeated everything.

I passed the half-full bottle of Dewar's to Brian. Everyone else knew not to ask. They could drink whatever the hell they wanted. The scotch was reserved. For some reason, he had an unusual intensity to him. A fiery passion edged his eyes and words. He motioned for me to hold back and let the others get ahead. He handed the bottle back, shaking his head.

"What's up?" I asked, staring ahead. We had just gotten a new employee. She wasn't exactly a supermodel, but she had a little hitch in her giddy up that I couldn't stop staring at. Plus, she didn't despise my existence, which was a welcome change...

"It's payday tomorrow," he said. His stare would have made Mike Tyson pause. "I know you're leaving soon, kid. You need to listen."

Leaving? What? I had barely formed that idea in my head.

How does he know?

Then he began to speak. Hard sentences, emphatically pronounced, demandingly delivered. He shared lessons he'd learned from jail: how to throw a correct punch, do a proper push up, and ways to tell when someone is lying to you. He told me about his life as a young man, particularly about some of the relationships he'd had. How he had gotten hosed in his first marriage. He lined out his philosophy, how to apply meditation and stoicism to my life, and talked about how the removal of the ego can lead to joy and freedom. How we, as men, are born to endure pain. And, most importantly, why it is paramount to anything else we will learn in life that we take the 'High Road.'

As we talked, others occasionally checked in. The new girl reached into my pocket and stole a cigarette. We ignored them. It was impossible to miss the power of his presence, how much he wanted me to avoid the pain and horror that he had experienced. There was a grim desperation to his words. He was trying to change the trajectory of my life through sheer force of will. A large bonfire had sprung up nearby. I could see the hard lines of his face written in flickering, sputtering light.

I ate up every word. My soul knew these were some of the greatest truths that I was likely to hear. If only I had actually implemented those ideals... But that is not how it goes. We all learn at our own pace and in our own way. We become strong by making the mistakes that shape us and passing on that knowledge to the next person in line. It is up to them to actually do the work. I was listening, but I was not ready to admit that I was already beat. Childish ideals of life and love still clung to the peripherals. I wanted to get lucky, not roll up my sleeves and commit to the undertaking. The bottle was empty and the fire was dying when he ran out of steam.

"You hear me, you little shit? The High Road. The fucking HIGH ROAD. You take it. No matter what."

Yeah, Old Man. I hear you.

The next day, we collected our checks and walked the four miles to the highway. It only took fifteen minutes with our thumbs out before an ancient, rust-covered F-150 pulled over. Brian high-fived the old woman in the passenger seat as we passed, then jumped in the bed of the truck. I followed, barely having time to zip up my hoodie and lean back against the window before the truck started racing down the two-lane highway. The rain was still falling but the cab shielded us from most of it.

He was talking to me, yelling through the wind and shaking his head with emphasis. I couldn't hear a word, so I pointed to my ear, shrugged, and laid down on the bare metal below. After a few minutes, he pushed my side with the flask and I took a long, slow pull.

There is a special kind of magic to riding in the back of a truck, watching the world go by. You are living in the flicker, completely at the mercy of life and the universe. A stag choosing that moment to sprint across the highway would mean certain death. The howling wind and rubber meeting asphalt create a deafening cacophony. You are lost in the tumult and turmoil of existence; a flea riding on the back of the great buffalo of life. The sense of scale and impermanence is never stronger. You are caught between here and there, always nowhere, yet somehow viscerally *present* in the movement. You are both lost and found, a human beta-testing wave-particle duality, real and tangible, illusory and imaginary. Here. There. Off. On.

Off.

The sun poked out. For a moment, everything seemed hopeful and bright. I drifted off into thought, thinking of where I wanted to go next. South. Definitely South. It was too damn cold there. A glimmer of aspiration made its way through the thick, waterlogged limbs, waving as we passed.

The ride came to a quick end on the outside of town. Most folks are just as eager to drop off hitchhikers as they are to pick them up. I tried to hand them 20 bucks and they politely refused. As I turned back, Brian was standing there with his arm outstretched. He had his pack on. He had something he needed to do, evidently.

Something was off. The whole scene felt rushed, unnecessarily uncomfortable. I shook it off as we shook hands, then parted ways. I yelled over my shoulder that he better pick up some more scotch for tomorrow. He grinned as he turned the corner.

I walked a few miles to the Walmart parking lot where I was meeting a man about a car. It was a cheap, dented, and well-used Honda Civic. The thing looked like it had been angrily beaten, multiple times, with a baseball bat. I opened the hood and prepared for the worst... but was shocked to find that the engine was immaculate. The guy was going on about all of the things he had swapped out, how he had never gotten to any of the body work, blah blah blah. I had already bought it in my mind. We haggled for a few minutes, then shook, and I pulled out a wad of cash.

"You mean, right now?" he said.

Yeah, man. Right now.

I drove straight to the DMV and had it registered and insured within the hour. There was something growing in the base of my spine. A restless, uncomfortable itch. It pulsed and vibrated. I tried calling Brian, but his number had been disconnected.

I stopped by the liquor store myself, then drove the same patch of road we had ridden across earlier. That already seemed like a lifetime ago. Something had happened that I couldn't sense or define. It felt as if I had bought a ticket but didn't know what it was for, where it was to, or whose name was on it. As I pulled into the parking lot of the lodge, all of the other employees were outside smoking. The shade they were throwing at me would have blunted Patch Adams's enthusiasm.

I didn't care anymore. Fuck 'em. I was free.

I flew up to the bunkroom, scotch in hand. I didn't have work till the next evening. Brian's bunk was by the window and the heater. I ran over to it, already unscrewing the cap, thinking of a joke I had heard on the radio... Then I noticed that his stuff was gone. The blanket on the bed had been changed and neatly folded. On the pillow was a note, written in crayon, with the penmanship of an insane, sugar-high child. It was definitely from Brian. It read:

"Reserved for Samson!"

It took a few moments for the reality to hit. The new girl poked her head in. She had been looking for both of us, hoping to see Brian before he left. Evidently, I was the last to have heard the news. I unscrewed the cap on the bottle and offered it to her. She grimaced and shook her head.

"So, he's gone?" I asked.

She hesitated, nodding, then stared at her shoes. "It's not even dinnertime," she muttered.

More for me.

A flow of questions began pouring from my head, down my spine, and into my chest. Why does everyone always leave? Am I unlovable? How am I supposed to deal with this place all alone? Why the fuck does everyone who needs advice keep *giving me* so much advice! The speed of my breath increased and rapidly became furious hyperventilation. The girl placed her hand on my shoulder.

Damn. Damn. Damn!

I took another pull from the bottle and fled the room. Something told me to get to the pools. There was too much debris... A dam had formed... I needed to wash it out...

I didn't bother with swim trunks. I stepped from the changing room in my boxers and jumped in the closest pool. I closed my eyes, and leaned back against the slick, polished cement. For once, the rain cleared. I could feel the sun across my face. It was like having someone speak Mandarin to me before my morning coffee. I breathed in deeply, then released. And again. And again...

After some time, I felt ripples against my chest. I must have dozed off. I opened my eyes to a dream. Sitting across from me was a young woman. Her face was beautiful enough to start a war with Troy. She had curves in all of the best places. It took a stronger will than I knew I possessed to keep my eyes level and off of the black bikini top...

She was staring right at me. I turned and looked behind me, then around the pool, then back to her. There was no one else around. I pointed to my chest and feigned shock. She smiled and pushed a strand of bright blonde hair away from her face, then slipped across the bench, holding out her hand.

Without thinking, I gently pulled it to my lips and kissed it. We talked for a while, and made plans to get drinks later that evening. As I rose from the pool, the woman stared at my glistening, pale body. Then she blew me a kiss.

When I reached my bunkroom, two new employees were unpacking their things. Both were as young as me, impressionable, and starry-eyed. They were the new waiters, hustling to get ready for their shift that night. It didn't take a genius to figure out what that meant.

"Do you like scotch?" I asked. Both of them shook their heads from side to side.

I gave them the cold shoulder. They weren't worth my time. Within minutes, my laptop was open, a broad set of tabs open to various jobs around the country. With quick, decided claps of the keys, I rattled off a slew of applications. Mindless, boring repetition, just like waiting tables... I was just about to set it down when an email arrived. It was the manager of a restaurant in Crater Lake National Park. He wanted to do an interview the following day. I set it up for noon and slammed the laptop triumphantly.

My date went extremely well, which was how I found myself lying face-up in the back of a black VW van. This was a newer version than Andy's, with updated furnishings and the gleaming polish of what she assured me was a fully working kitchen. The faint rattling of raindrops overlaid two sets of heavy, slowing breaths. Thick clouds of vapor commingled with the smoke from her cigarette. She looked at me, winked again, and gave me a quick kiss on the cheek. I understood what she meant.

As I slid the door closed behind me, I saw the manager of the restaurant standing by the door to the lodge. A look of impatience was plastered below his bald pate. He was tapping his foot and slamming a pile of papers against his hands. He thrust them out in my direction.

"These are write-ups." He said. His face was flushed. Maybe he had some scotch of his own. "One for tardiness, another for using the pools during the daytime, the last for fraternizing..."

Blah, blah, blah.

I stood there and took the verbal onslaught. It was a jarring shift to the pleasantness I had been enjoying for the past few hours. When he finished his list, he dove into my attitude problems and how he was going to have to let me—

"Okay," I said, and started to walk up the steps.

"Okay?!" he replied, his face reddening even further. He looked like a middle-aged tomato left to wither on the vine. "That's it?!"

I nodded and kept moving. I slipped into my room to the sounds of snoring employees. The new kids were still up, the bright lights of their cell phones silhouetting their faces. I laid down quickly, popped in my ear plugs, and tried to process the day. There was no use. When I awoke the next morning there was a notice on the door telling me to vacate by 5 p.m.

The black van was gone when I pulled out of the parking lot. I did another circle just to make sure. The rest of the morning was one long cigarette and a pile of empty coffee cups on the passenger seat. Towns passed, all of them painted in dull, weathered blues and greens, tacitly resisting the domination of gray.

There was no cell service. I began to pick up speed. It was almost noon when I spotted a payphone, standing alone in a small shard of grass, its back to a broad expanse of coastline. Just beyond was the turnoff onto the bridge across the Columbia River. There was no way... Surely these had all disappeared long ago?

I wiped off the receiver and was surprised by an active dial tone. I called my new manager and watched the waves fight the howling wind. The sun glared. Cars whipped down the highway. I told him where I was and he laughed. I could start immediately.

"There is a fire at the east end of the park, so you'll want to take the north entrance, just off Highway 138. The detour road is higher than normal, the construction crews are using gravel..."

"Okay, 97 down to...did you say higher than normal?"

"Yeah, is that a problem?" he said, still chuckling.

"No, sir. I always take the High Road."

The phone ran out of time and cut off. I wasn't concerned. A lit cigarette appeared in my mouth. The ocean fought and raged, roaring at one and all. The salty air prickled the nape of my neck. Something was still burning deep within me and it wasn't the Marlboro. It was a pulsing, grinding... need. I had to find something. Someone, it, where, when, mine, yours... infinity. I knew something was shifting. A decision had been made, a deal negotiated.

I started the engine and took off down the highway.

12

CRATERS OF THE MOON

Residual heat clung to my heels as I worked the pedals. The gears shifted smoothly. In the passenger seat was an open laptop, half-buried by empty coffee cups and a pile of leather-bound notebooks. Puffs of ash gently billowed from the overflowing ashtray, the spent butts jiggling with the whims of the cracked pavement.

I was on the road again. The job had ended less abruptly this time. Something still burned deep within, a scorching heat constantly flared from the inner core, erupting silently on my face, legs, and arms.

My hair had grown long, despite the corporate grooming standards. I could feel the stack of Polaroids piercing my left ass cheek, mementos from a young woman who had seen more in me than I could. It had been too good, too pure. She had treated me... well. It didn't fit the narrow, rusting lens that obscured the unspoiled wilderness we had danced in.

I'd seen my father, taking the woman and the Polaroid camera to his house. It was the first time I'd been to one of his homes since Myrtle Creek. Without thinking, I'd grabbed our passports from the glove box before we went inside. He'd offered me a beer. That time, I refused.

Things fell apart quickly after that. I had everything. A supportive, close-knit workplace. Oodles of cash. Close friends, secret handshakes, nighttime adventures... even my boss liked me. She said I reminded her of her son. I couldn't process any of it. The world of love and acceptance was too foreign, as if I was a stowaway on a cruise liner, and any moment I would be found out and tossed overboard. The general manager was shocked when I put in my notice.

"But you look so happy!" he said.

The highway stretched ahead. I despised maps, especially electronic ones. You're supposed to be lost. That was the only thing I knew to be true. I had no idea what I was heading toward. I had a tent, enough gear to survive in the woods, and a thin roll of foam to keep my bones off the ground. The wad of cash in the console was enough to make it to the Atlantic. It would have to be enough.

Before leaving the state, I'd driven up to see my brother. As always, it was bittersweet. On the outside, he was warm and welcoming, but his unease was obvious.

We did what we always did. Cartoons reflected off of the bongs on the battered coffee table. We ashed our cigarettes in the ever-expanding field of empty beer cans and caught up on things. It was easy to drown the gulf between us with mindless chatter. The same old jokes evoked the same old terse laughter. We ordered pizza and passed out early, brightly colored characters dancing across the white walls of his dingy apartment.

The following morning, he handed me some brownies. His wry expression spoke volumes. It was a look that said, "I am going to start laughing as soon as you leave and keep laughing till you call to cuss me out."

I wasn't thinking about them in particular. I was thinking of my ex-girlfriend, my ex-friends, my ex-home, my ex-father, Brian's words, and the beautiful woman I had just left in tears. I needed to run. I hugged him, jumped in the car like it had a shotgun window, and raced toward the highway. My car leapt onto the onramp, a bridled horse snorting and yawing, then lunging through the gate in a frenzied attempt to pound the dirt ahead.

A virulent storm battered the car as I crossed Highway 20. I was sluiced through the barren canyons, then slapped on the ass and abruptly forgotten. The sun broke through as soon as I crossed the border, rising high above the Idaho plains. I drove too fast, recklessly accelerating through the curves. East. I had to get East. Miles passed.

The campground was called Craters of the Moon. The name checked out. I set up camp, then went hiking and exploring. The sun set brilliantly, casting deep oranges, magenta, and thick browns on the dark clouds in the distance. Just before dark, I made sandwiches around a small fire, then pulled out my guitar and played as I diligently worked through a 12-pack.

My worst decisions are usually made in a vacuum, that airy gap between reason and coincidence. It was no surprise, then, that after a few beers the brownies my brother had given me started to sound like a great idea. I ate the first one and thought nothing of it. An hour passed. It was getting late, and I wasn't feeling anything, so I ate the other one.

The embers of the fire began to wink out. The cold came in one oppressive wave, gripping my elbows and biting my earlobes. I grabbed my book, a bag of chips, and my remaining beers, then jumped into the tent. With the sleeping bag pulled up to my neck, I felt cozy and at peace. I knew that the worst thing that could happen was to oversleep and force the Park Ranger to kick me out.

I was wrong. I had a really good book series with me, a stack of page-turners that had me hooked, line and sinker. I ate and drank mechanically as the pages whipped by. Shards of expelled potato chips were spread across everything as if the bag had been violently murdered with a chainsaw. This was really funny to me. *Really* funny. I tried to set down my last beer and somehow it shot upwards, spewing its remaining contents everywhere.

Oh, boy.

More pages turned. Fits of giggles and deep sighs shook my frame. I could *breathe*. Above my head was the open expanse, the sweeping tract of the galaxy exploding overhead, an almost complete and total silence quivering around the thin nylon mesh above. I was acutely aware that I was on the right path. I felt like I had finally made the right decisions. For the briefest of interludes, I was at peace.

It didn't last long.

It turns out the worst thing that could happen in that instance was a thunderstorm. I had fallen asleep in placid stillness, the drugs and alcohol working together in a beautiful symphony that lulled me into dreamland. I woke up to a thunderclap that cracked the world in half. Residual energy snapped through the air. The sound was enough to wake the dead, which was probably close to my current state. Echoes reverberated between the rocks. The rain crashed down in a flood.

Oh, shit.

Flood. Lightning. And my tent was open... fat, overladen drops pushed through the exposed mesh, faster than should have been possible. I rolled out of my sleeping bag, crunching chip shards and beer cans, and lunged through the narrow exit. It took just under a minute to clip the corners of the rainfly and ram home the stakes. I threw myself back inside the tent just in time. What I had thought was a deluge was just an appetizer. The storm earnestly intensified.

The waves of water that mercilessly fell from the sky made a sound against the poor, innocent nylon that resembled a high school cheer team pounding slapsticks against a railing. Every fifteen seconds, there was a flash of lightning accompanied by the almost immediate clap of thunder that rattled bones. I felt like a tuning fork left unattended near a floor-mounted subwoofer. It took me at least fifteen minutes to realize that I wasn't dreaming. It took me even longer to realize that I might be in danger.

I've been in a lot of intense weather events in my life. The obvious thing to do is to avoid panicking. Typically, it sounds and feels way worse than it is. This was not one of those cases. This was a flash flood in the middle of nowhere, punctuated by a lightning storm directly over my head. The hair on my head was sticking straight up, which meant the lightning strikes were close. Really close.

It was then, in the full fury of Nature's wrath, that the brownies kicked in. I lay there in my damp mummy bag and stared wide-eyed at the outside of my tent. My hands reached out in both directions and found... my last beer. It was still a quarter full. I chugged it and lit a damp cigarette. Then the hallucinations started.

At first, I thought that aliens were here. Little green or brown men, descended from the heavens, bringing with them the fury of the universe. And these little invaders wanted my butthole. Man, I was going to get probed *for sure*. It was a nightmarish fever dream. Aliens! Here! Now!

Fuck!

Suddenly, I wasn't so sure. Current raged through my veins. My blood swam with the air. My soul was raw and naked, cut open for the universe to pour into. With each concussive crash, small, prong-headed devils danced along the wildly flapping sides of my tent. I heard squeaking... me. I was *squeaking*. What had I been thinking? Was I really as fearless as I thought? Why had I left that job?

Man, I really don't want to get probed...

It was about this time that the water started to pick up the tent and rapidly push me across the campsite. Ever wonder why they put those big logs on the sides of the concrete pads that you camp on? They aren't just there for looks. They are there to stop your tent from physically moving down into the water drainage canals carving up the middle of the campgrounds. At least, I know that's what mine were for. And in between covering my head to protect against the alien/demon/monsters—*don't touch the sides, don't touch the sides*—the squeaks turned to howls. Primal. Feral.

I lit a last cigarette and waited for the end.

It never came. As the hours passed, I'd given up on trying to stay dry. I was a salamander. Braving demon spears and tractor beams, I put my back to the onrush, placed my feet against the logs, and accepted my fate.

I adamantly believed that I was an atheist back then. I believed that no loving God deserved reverence for allowing the criminal shortage of dopamine and serotonin in my brain. I was also a master of blaming this nonexistent God for all of my troubles. And yet, with my neck and nuts soaking in a baptism of cold, red mud, I prayed.

Please. Please. Not my butthole...

Centuries passed. As they always do, the storm passed. The sky's silence was met with the sounds of gentle burbling from the ground. I began to peel out of my sopping nest, and found that three of my limbs had gone completely numb. I reached up to the small pouch dangling from the center. With trembling hands, I pulled the pack apart. And there, in between several damp ones, were a pair of perfectly dry cigarettes.

Thank you.

It only took ten minutes to have everything pulled out of the tent. The campground looked roughly the same as the day before. A small mound of mud, piled against where my feet had been, was the only evidence of the epic struggle that had occurred.

Movement was agony. My hands and toes began to send icy tendrils of pain up to the mangled grey matter above. I couldn't tell if the water on my cheeks was from my hair or eyes. I didn't bother packing my things neatly, instead tossing them all into the back seat. I left the heat on full blast and stood watching the sunrise in the distance.

Slowly, I peeled my clothes from my waterlogged skin. I was bad at being amphibious. Every hair on my mammalian body stood straight up, reaching toward the slim slit of sun... When I turned back around, the windows had fogged completely.

As I slowly drove around the narrow asphalt loop, other campers were starting to emerge from their trailers. Every eye stared, their amusement barely hidden. I hoped that the gas station I had passed the day before had a pot of coffee on. As I passed the booth at the entrance, the two park rangers sat staring, their crisp brown uniforms a stark contrast to the crumbling walls around them. Both were laughing and waving. I stared straight ahead and hoped that they couldn't see the flush in my cheeks.

I turned right onto the highway, headed east. The engine hummed and purred, well-oiled and spoiling for a run. The highway was smooth, gently curving through the high plains. Without warning, the sun broke through the scattered clouds, still pregnant, dark, and heavy. The light cast across the dusty dashboard. My cheeks dried. The gas station did have a fresh pot on. A large older woman poured me a cup and handed it to me. Concern radiated from her eyes and framed the thick jowls of her face.

"On the house, young man. Long night?"

I nodded, too humbled to speak, then walked out the door. I drove the rest of the day, my mind stilled and empty. That night, I got the nicest hotel I could find.

13

STAG

Dust rose in small plumes from where I'd slid down the parched, lifeless soil. The tree-well was a thick divot bored into a broad scree field. My left hand held a medium-sized boulder, my right an exposed root. Normally, it is a solid practice to avoid 'plant holds' of any kind—they can't be trusted. But my body had a solid practice of its own that was currently taking precedence.

The campsite was a short jaunt from the main path. A goat trail spurred off and dropped into a handful of surviving trees, all bent at odd angles in their own respective battles with gravity. I was headed up toward Paintbrush Divide, a narrow, sloping meander through one of the Grand Tetons. These massive outcroppings, mountains made by long-dead Gods to spite the sky, dominated the surrounding earth for hundreds of miles in all directions.

I was less than a gnat to a place such as this. I might as well have been an amoeba, crawling along the ravaged skin of a massive host...

Earlier that morning, the ranger had glanced at my extra-large coffee cup with a bemused smile. He asked if I had ever camped before. It took all of my willpower not to forcefully remove his front teeth with the back of my hand. I said nothing until he asked where I wanted to pitch my tent. I'd replied simply:

"Alone."

I spent the rest of the morning storming up the trail, burning aggression and sorrow by planting my boot heels into the loose rock. Moody and powerful music blared through my ear buds as I passed other hikers. My feet still burned, and not from the pace. I'd stopped charging my phone a week before. I couldn't bear to hear her voice again. There was only one thing to do: walk. Far. Ideally, somewhere that most people wouldn't go. I reached my destination hours before I had intended to.

The campsite sat astride a recent rockslide. One of the mountains in the distance had evidently thrown a tantrum at some point. Countless tons of mud and stone had swept through the narrow valley, mauling everything in its path. The trail wound steeply, dropped into a bowl, then carried on along the ridgeline above. Aside from the scant trees over my tent, there was little to obscure myself from the prying eyes of the hikers I had passed earlier. When duty called, I'd had to get creative. Into the hole I went.

The sun was still high in the sky. The body will rapidly acclimatize to the whims of the natural world. I'd been camping for weeks, rising with the sun and laying down soon after dark. These weren't the only mountains that I had sought out. The quiet of the wild beckoned.

Without knowing it consciously, I was ravenous for the greatest of wisdoms. The breath of the world whispered on the winds, the highest summits of experience cast across broad swathes of color and fortitude. I was running completely on coffee and instinct. My soul knew that I needed a higher perspective. I had to find a way to talk to my Creator.

I had questions.

No answers were forthcoming in that tree well, though. The sunbaked root splintered as I pushed off. My heels dug deep into the stones and soil beneath. I dipped behind the roots and thrust myse—

Not two feet away, grazing on a patch of grass, was a stag. The beast was massive, at least eight well-defined prongs bursting from its skull. I stopped, mid-breath. It stopped, mid-chew. Fear plunged into my spine, a spinal tap of the ice-cold breath of Hell, my veins bulging and pulsing with the efforts of my furiously beating heart. Time passed. The beast began to slowly paw the ground in front of it. It huffed once. I could feel the air it expelled on my exposed thigh.

I jumped backward into the hole without looking. Fortune must have smiled, because I didn't land where I had just been preoccupied or on any of the dozens of football-sized rocks dotting the well. I backed away quickly. When I reached the other side, I scrambled up the embankment in an undignified scurry.

The stag hadn't moved. It stood resolute—somehow more powerful than mere seconds before. Slowly, and possibly deliberately, it turned to one side and began to gradually fade toward my campsite. There was a sense of purpose and determination to the movements. I took this as the beast being territorial. 'Alone' didn't seem like such a great idea any more.

I found a boulder and lounged in the sun. My legs were taut and well-muscled. The skin of my belly was white enough to scare away predators of all kinds. I tried to breathe, to feel the world around me... until the stag began to sniff around the edges of my tent. Without thinking, I was there in a flash. I had to. This was a multi-day trek. I couldn't have anything getting into my food bag.

The beast didn't listen for a moment. It traipsed and trotted across the human-demarcated area in a clear example of who the Big Cheese was. I did the only thing I could do: pulled out my camera and started taking photos. Something about the whole thing seemed familiar.

Eventually, the pronged asshole purposefully ambled out of the camp and down the scree field. Somewhere near the bottom of the scree field was a waterfall, narrow, short, and pure. I'd passed it earlier that day. No doubt this beast had worked up quite the thirst intimidating me. I watched it retreat down the hill, massive hind legs carefully picking their way along. The tail, luminescent white and standing tall, wagged a bit, as if to say hello.

What the hell was that?

The rest of the day was spent cooking meals, resting in my hammock, and bear-proofing my camp. I had learned my lesson working in Yosemite, where the wildlife outnumbered the humans, and if you left anything out, you were guaranteed to have a black bear in your tent. My food bag hung high up in the branches of the nearest tree, a rope tied to the roots below.

I should have been afraid. Or at least had a healthy respect and trepidation for the wilderness. It just never occurred. I was numb, devoid of serotonin and dopamine, and regularly did everything I could to bring about my own demise. Despite hundreds of examples to the contrary, I still clung to the notion that I was an atheist.

They were all bullshit—God, the Creator, spirits. All of it. Foolish notions. I hated them. And yet, all of 'it' was God's fault. It also never occurred to me that *hating* a higher power is still believing. You can't hate something that doesn't exist. I lay back into the nylon seams and rocked back and forth on the hammock, chain-smoking and taking nips from a flask. I asked questions aloud that I knew had no chance of being answered.

It was all a goddamn scam. I was just a pawn to be used, a body to be ruined. It was better to just get it over with. No one would ever love me. There was no point to any of the things that I did.

What am I doing here?

Nightfall came with little fanfare. The encroaching dark took the light inch by inch, second by second. Fires weren't allowed, so there was no torch to hold back whatever else dwelled nearby. I watched the stars for a long time, then crawled into my sleeping bag and quickly fell asleep.

I awoke to a loud huffing directly behind my head. Something was pawing the ground and softly pacing, sounds that were barely audible over a furiously racing heart. It now occurred to me to be afraid. The 'myth of the tent,' where some people can imagine the thin fabric and aluminum poles as an insulated and defensible structure, was not one of my weaknesses. I knew how exposed I was. A squeak came from somewhere. Right, I was alone. It came from me. I knew I had to yell, to make noise, to do my best to seem big...

Another squeak ripped from my lips. Maybe it sounded like a roar to one of the nearby mice. Maybe they would band together and come to my rescue...

The huffing continued, thick, guttural rumbles. The tent flap suddenly bulged. No more options. Instead, action. An idea came to me. I ripped the headlamp out of the corner pocket and turned it on behind me. It cast my shadow across the broad expanse of the tent. Then I dug deep into my solar plexus; into my guts. Into my nuts. This one sounded much like a roar. Still a little squeaky, but definitely an improvement. For a moment, silence reigned. Then the tent flap bulged again...

So this is it, huh?

I did the only thing I could do. I reached up to the dangling pack of cigarettes, pulled one out, and lit it. After inhaling deeply, I started talking.

A torrent of words poured out. Dreams. Wishes. Laments. Grievances. Even a quote from Tom Petty. I talked, spitting words machine-gun style, trying to get it all out before the end came. The soft sounds of movement wrapped around and around. There was no telling which way to point the headlamp. I had to simply accept that I had done everything I could do.

"I'M SORRY!" I screamed. "I'M FUCKING SORRY, OK!? I just wanted—"

But there were more footfalls now. Stamping, stronger than before. Louder huffing. Something jumped and came down on the corner of the tent. It was gone just as fast. I lit up another cigarette. Smoke seeped out of the rainfly, creeping toward whatever was out there. Then there was silence.

An eternity passed as I sat, chain-smoking and finishing the flask that was supposed to last the entire trip. My sleeping bag was pulled up to my chin, my back straighter than it had ever been. I couldn't touch the walls of the tent. The walls were lava. And there was something out there that wasn't scared of me.

At some point, I summoned the courage to open the tent flap. I threw out a lit cigarette first; I figured that the smoke might be just enough to deter an animal. It was worth a shot. I grabbed my headlamp and rushed forward. My feet were numb as my heart beat at a merciless pace. I whirled, trying to look everywhere at once and, naturally, seeing nothing. As this realization dawned, I began to slowly turn the light in a circle, seeking the source of the noises. There was nothing.

I was alone.

I slept poorly that night and got up with the sun. I emerged from the tent into a crisp morning, dew caking rocks and tufts of grass alike. I spotted a great deal of tracks. Some focused on my tent, a loose oval formed around it, with some right at the entrance. Some were farther out, near the hammock, coming from the bottom of the scree field.

Now, I am no master tracker, but I have spent a considerable amount of time in the wilderness. I have seen my fair share of tracks. And some of them on the ground around me looked distinctly like hooves. Big ones. And the others looked a hell of a lot like paws.

The coffee made itself, a grim understanding taking hold as the water boiled and the instant blend soaked into the pan. Some of my questions had been answered. I just didn't know which ones they were. I had the key. Now all I needed was the lock.

As soon as my coffee and jerky were finished, I packed up camp and started up the trail. The morning greeted me with swiftly darting birds, cold streams, and butterflies. Each step took me further into myself. I placed one foot in front of the other and tried to smile. A startling realization burst into my frame of awareness. I was alive. And I was happy about it.

As I came across a broad switchback, I could see the scree field below. It was even more impressive from a high vantage. The amount of force that could create this much devastation... truly remarkable. It didn't take long to pick out where my campsite had been the night before. It was the only place that had been left untouched by the rock fall. My eyes drifted up the slope... and standing there, resolute and tall, was the stag. I stared, dumbfounded.

He stared right back. I could feel his eyes boring into whatever was left of my soul, without judgment. I knew then that he had saved me. I knew other things too; things I couldn't define. The only one that seemed clear was that the answers would come. One foot in front of the other. One step at a time.

I waved at The Stag and grinned. Instead of waving back, he turned away and headed back down the hill. I took that as a good sign. I turned up the trail and kept walking.

14

SUNSHINE

As soon as I arrived, I was hired at a restaurant in Vermont. It was short-lived. The manager wanted to personally count my tips each evening. I hadn't even bothered to fill out a W-2. It was cash out the door, "This isn't working out," and "Thanks for coming all of this way." The feeling was mutual. A wink at the cook, apron on the counter, and then it was back to smoking cigarettes in the car.

I'd rented a room at an inn down the road. It was a massive structure with three wings, set in a U-shape at the base of a steep, thickly wooded hill. It was almost 'Leafer Season,' so the occasional couple stopped through for a night or two. But I barely noticed the other guests. I'd been given an entire wing to myself.

I soon went to work for the innkeepers. They had a fondness for me that I couldn't comprehend. It was a foreign concept. I couldn't fathom why anyone would want me around for anything.

I spent my days painting, cutting down trees, and chopping wood. At dusk, I would sit on the steps of the broad stone porch, writing poems until they called me in for dinner. Weeks passed with a smooth rhythm. Time was measured in clear nights spent gazing at the stars and early mornings drinking coffee in a nearby thicket. When they offered me a long-term position, I panicked.

As soon as I was finished for the day, I ran to my room and got on my laptop. I found another job on Craigslist within minutes. It was a barbecue stand that specialized in pulled pork and breakfast sandwiches. Fifteen minutes after I sent the email, my phone rang. I packed my bag as he told me the details.

I awoke at 5 a.m. the next morning and did my best to sneak down the creaking staircase. The trunk of my car closed with a soft click at the same time that the front door opened. The innkeeper walked up to me, wearing pajamas and a knowing smile. He held out a massive cup of coffee, which I gratefully accepted. He plied me with jokes and asked when I'd be back. I couldn't answer. My feet burned as I shook his hand.

By 8 a.m., my tent was set up in the middle of the fairground, next to my new employer's massive RV. I was a cook again. My morning consisted of brewing coffee and making egg sandwiches. The rest of the day was a blur of faces, a line stretching deep into the middle of the midway.

Between pulling chunks of pork apart, whipping together heaps of nachos, and ramming potatoes through a slicer, I instantly became the single greatest detriment to the gastrointestinal health of New England. In the background, the whistling, clanging bells, and mechanical contrivances of the carnival rang out. The constant tramping of thousands of visitors spewed massive plumes of dust that fell everywhere. Obscuring. Choking...

Three days passed like this. We cooked, cracked jokes, and threw ourselves at the work. Then the man's family arrived. Well, not *his* family. His girlfriend's family. Five children and two grandparents in tow, she brusquely strode into the main trailer and planted a wet kiss on the man's cheek. There was something there, a grim fatality in her movements... it was hard to meet her eyes. I knew them. They held the unmistakable gleam of hopelessness.

Four of the five children darted off into the fair and only returned infrequently to collect money from my boss. One, however, quickly took a shine to me and assigned herself the job of my assistant. I didn't mind. Something about her made me smile. Maybe it was the way that she dropped every peeled potato that she picked up, or the way that she giggled at the sounds the nacho cheese made when it was pumped. It didn't matter. She was a bright light in a very dark tunnel. She told me her name multiple times, but I forgot it.

I called her Sunshine.

It was Saturday when they arrived. The Big Day. I'd been up at the crack of dawn, peeling potatoes and tearing scalding-hot pork into smaller pieces. This was my life, the path that I had chosen. It was tolerable because it was for such a short duration. I knew that everything ended, but this ended sooner than anything else. It was a commitment I knew I could make.

I tossed the last piece of hog in the bin and stripped off my gloves. When I turned to the coffee pot for a fresh cup, Sunshine was sitting there, her feet dangling off of a case of bottled water. I watched as she twirled her toes, reaching high, toying with the swirling dust. Thick smoke, heavy with the scent of charred meat, barged into the open doors with every stray bit of breeze.

As I poured caffeinated bean water into a massive Styrofoam cup, she handed me a gummy. It was some kind of fruit snack, the kind that only kids eat. I hadn't had one in over a decade. Down the hatch it went. She beamed and handed me a handful, telling me that while she was almost out of them, someday her Mommy will go to the bank, pull money out of the shiny machine, and then she'll have more to share. She giggled again as I chewed the bounty I had received. The gummies were heavenly. She perked up and looked me straight in the eye, then told me that her favorite color is pink and purple.

"Black," I said, without being asked.

"That's not a color!"

"Don't I know it..."

I stepped outside and lit a cigarette. My boss and the woman's father joined me. The company of fools. This was presumably our last break for hours. We toasted our coffee, then stepped inside. A line was already forming.

The rush started and never let up. It was a brutal slog; a catastrophic misuse of carbohydrates; a steaming, sagging procession of cardboard boats passed from hand to hand. The cash box filled, over and over. Fryers sizzled, trays of pork emptied, and nacho cheese splattered the walls. My assistant stayed at my heels, kicking me when I forgot to hand her bits of food, slipping gummies into my hand when I sighed.

Sometime around lunch, it came out that it was the woman's fortieth birthday. There she was, choking on dust at a run-down fair, hustling pork and nine-dollar buckets of fries. Living the Dream. I also learned that she had no job of her own. As she hollered back orders, a lot of things became clear.

The gleam I had recognized, the strain in Sunshine's face, the tension inside the trailer... it was an obvious crisis, the distinct obliteration of everything she'd hoped and dreamed for. They were like lost luggage on the carousel, hoping to be claimed by mistake. As the heat of the day rose, my boss and the woman began to trade thinly veiled barbs.

I kept on babysitting. Sunshine was better company, anyway. Her favorite type of cloud was 'fluffy.' That's what she had named her cat. She was a stark reminder of everything I had lost over the past year: naïveté, innocent optimism, and hope in the face of grim realities.

She tried to reach her hands up onto the face of the grill. I darted a greasy hand out and caught her along the armpits, ruining her pink shirt. For a moment, I held her suspended in the air. Chaos reigned around us. She giggled as I set her down.

It all fell apart during the Dinner Rush. The terse back-and-forth between my boss and the birthday girl had escalated, boiling over like the overworked fryers. Soon, the two adults were openly shouting, digging into one another, both heated yet somehow impassive. The coldness was jarring. This wasn't a passionate exchange. It was a business deal, a stoically transactional arrangement.

Sometime around 10 p.m., the line finally dissipated. The couple had broken up. The woman was homeless. The man was sitting outside, chain-smoking. Sunshine stood, anxiously glued to my hip. The rest of the family had returned and were now looking at one another, no doubt wondering when the hell they could get out of there. I knew, with startling clarity, that I would never see any of them again.

I hoped, for their sake, that this was true.

The fight restarted and spilled out behind the trailer. The grandparents' voices joined the fray. I now had five charges, all staring up at me with wide eyes. I did the only thing I could do. I made them nachos and moonwalked across the greasy floor. As the yelling reached a fever pitch, I snuck a hand out of the front window and closed the gate. We'd made enough money that day. There was beer in the fridge. I helped myself to two of them and closed the back door as well.

There's only so much a man can do to keep kids distracted in a filthy barbecue stand. I chugged my beers and did my best. We made faces and danced, sliding back and forth across the floor. We tore up unused buns and tried to throw them in each other's mouths. The fear gleamed in their eyes. I couldn't save them. I couldn't save *anyone*...

"You hear me, you little shit? The High Road. The fucking HIGH ROAD..."

As soon as the shouting stopped, I grabbed another beer and went for the door. To my surprise, I had picked up a hitchhiker. Sunshine attached herself to my leg with the insistent grip of a climber on the last handhold before the top of the mountain. There was only one thing to do. As the door opened, I stepped out, handed the beer to my employer, picked up Sunshine by the armpits, and ran out into the fair.

Then she was flying. Superwoman. I held her above my head, keeping her as high above the ground as my skinny arms could manage. All the cares, fear, and concern melted from her face as if they had never existed. We whooped and howled, tearing off through the midway, carnies on either side laughing and goading us on. Everything dissolved into the sea of people flowing between the neon lights. We were dust, floating briefly on the bone-dry air, careless. She giggled and snorted, reminding me how to laugh a six-year-old's laugh. Behind us were the broken adults, carelessly throwing away the fleeting happiness of arrogance. In front of us were the flashing lights and the games of youth.

We tried them all. I learned quickly that I was really bad at tossing rings, but exceptional at throwing darts. I popped my last balloon and collected the pink teddy bear she selected. As I turned my face downwards, I could see her outstretched arms. I looked to the trailer we had left in the distance. Her grandfather stood there, hands on his hips, watching. I gave him a thumbs up, which he returned. Then I picked her up and set her on my shoulders.

Her little legs dangled down, and her teddy bear sat on top of my head. For a moment, she got to be off the ground. It is all we can ever ask for, the only thing we can ever strive to achieve—those moments where we can be children at the fair, soaring through the sky.

With one hand on her hip and the other on one of her frail, skinny ankles, I guided her through the fray. I saw other young children reaching their arms up to their respective adults. Her weight against gravity was nothing. My back was strong. I would never be able to support the weight of what she would inevitably fall back to when I let her go... but for now, it was enough. Her joy was boundless. Her laughter was everything. She giggled. She flew.

This was what I was here for.

I didn't know how alone I had been until that day. I'd had no idea how badly I'd needed to laugh and jump and talk about dinosaurs. I bought cotton candy. We rode the Tilt-a-Whirl. Bells chimed and whistles shrieked. Then it was time. I could hear her grandmother calling. As we neared the trailer, we spied her mother standing there, camera aloft. In the flicker of a flashing bulb, the world slowed down, waiting just a second for the two sun-faced kids to play superhero.

Amidst the oppressive heat and the overbearing cacophony of sounds, the dust cloud fell.

I let Sunshine down and she ran to her mother, showing off her new teddy bear. I walked around to the back end of the trailer. It was closed and locked. I knocked, and the man pounded across the metal floors. When he saw it was me, he relaxed and beckoned me in. We shared a beer and a cigarette, then he handed me a wad of cash and slapped my shoulder. I finished my beer quickly and started for the parking lot.

"Wait!" came the shrill cry. She was there before I finished turning around. Small hands gripped my waist. Her face buried itself into the thick flesh of my thighs. I knelt down and hugged her back.

"Thank you, sweetheart," I whispered. I felt something tugging at my pocket, but dismissed it. I stood, waved to the adults crowding behind, and got in my car.

I'd packed up the tent earlier that morning. As I waited for the engine to warm up, I pulled the roll of bills to count them. As I did, a wrapper fell out onto the floor. It was a package of some kind... a pack of gummies.

As I drove away, I popped the handful in my mouth. I was headed south. There was a job in New York, selling apple pie and pastries. A Tom Petty song came on the radio. A smile came to my lips as I began to sing.

15

MOUNT REYNOLDS

I have to jump.

I was half-crouched, half-sprawled across a vertical crack in the cliff face, my legs pinned to either side. There wasn't much rock between my legs and the precipitous drop below. As I watched, a small pebble shook loose from under my elbow and rolled off into space. It was still falling when I lost patience waiting for it to hit the ground.

I'd gotten 'cliffed out.' I couldn't move up or down on the rock face without putting myself in a bad spot. It had happened to a few of my friends a week before. They'd had to be airlifted out. My confidence in my own abilities was so high that I'd figured it could never happen to me. I also thought that climbing mountains by myself was a good idea. I wasn't in my right mind. I looked out at the horizon and thought about how I'd gotten there.

***

The bastards had stolen my car. The police had told me it happened all the time on the Reservation. My trusted steed had made it back and forth across the country, only to die, smoking and limping, on a desolate Montana highway. Its last service was to make it onto the safety of the shoulder before shuddering to a halt. I'd hitchhiked back to employee housing, looking back over my shoulder only once.

When I walked into the dorm, there'd been a note on my bed. It read, simply:

Call me. xxx

I stared at it for a long moment. The paper was hotel stationery. I had spent the night before looking for her, wondering why she wasn't answering her phone. I loved her. I didn't know what she loved.

A bottle sat, lidless and half full, on the desk I shared with my roommate. I took a long swig. And another. Then I crumpled the paper and threw it over my shoulder.

Something still burned under my feet and soul. I needed release. I couldn't feel the booze anymore. I couldn't feel anything. Food was just gas in the tank. Sleep was a necessary impediment to getting more work done. I was jaded, traumatized, and alone. Life had become a cruel joke with no punchline.

I knew that I was running out of time to find purpose and there were only two places I knew of to reconnect: the highway and the trail. The bastards had stolen my car. That left one other option.

I threw some food and water into my pack. There was a shuttle up to Logan Pass that left every fifteen minutes. I walked down the short dirt road to the highway. The tinges of summer had just started to seep through the cold clutches of spring. The snow had melted, but the wind still held ice underneath its palms.

A moose was bathing in the pond to my left. None of the other employees along the road looked up from their phones, the massive animal just feet away as they passed. It nonchalantly munched on whatever moose like to eat at the bottom of ponds.

I reached the bottom of the hill, still staring backwards at the beast. People flew from all over the world to witness them, and here we had one in our backyard. Bears were just as common. There was even a mob of wild horses that darted across the plains wherever they pleased. The Reservation had no fences.

The bus stop was a single signpost, slanted at a rakish angle, rusted almost completely through. I didn't even have time to light a cigarette before the shuttle appeared on the road ahead.

Climbing mountains was something I took lightly. There were so many of them, most with well-defined trails that led up to their peaks. I had already 'bagged' a half-dozen that season. As I crossed from the lightly populated trail toward the jutting peak, it quickly became clear that this one was different. There was no maintenance, flags, or markers. I had read the cliff notes on my phone as the bus wound up through the switchbacks of Going-to-the-Sun Road. Everything had seemed so simple. The farther up I went, however, the more lost I became.

Two hours later, I was hanging from a rock face, my backpack dangling from one shoulder. I was fit, lean, and lithe, with hands worn to the nubs from fights and climbs like this. Physically, it was easy. I was still not scared of death. It was the emotional part that I struggled with.

For a brief moment, I looked down. Thousands of feet below, massive rockfalls spread out in a broad expanse, sweeping outward in a grand display of ambivalence. I was nothing to this mountain. Not even a fly. I could fall and be crushed beneath countless tons, my name erased from memories with the snap of a finger, leaving only the briefest of dust prints. And for the first time in months, I felt something.

It was glorious.

I growled and started lunging forward. There was no cathartic release, no transcendental moment. Just a desperate thrust against gravity. I had to push upward, strive forward to the next handhold. The crumbling, 'jank' rock held for just long enough to get past. Pebbles, dirt, and chunks flew out with each movement. I was in a dangerous position, but there was no safe place to land. I didn't want to live or die, and I couldn't admit either one of them. One hand at a time. Upward.

The peak came suddenly. Mt. Reynolds has a relatively flat top, a stark reminder of the glaciers that carved out the surrounding landscape. Small rocks cascaded downward, rolling down across the rock face and down toward the waiting abyss. Then my hands found air, hips thrust forward, and a bellow tore from my lips.

I stood alone atop the mountain, looking out on the Crown of the Continent. The wind whipped, and a flash darted through the glacier-fed canyons and ravines pock-marking thickly wooded slopes. I looked to the south. Thick, black clouds hung menacingly over the entire expanse. The sun bravely assaulted the flanks of the massive thunderheads, to little effect and no avail. They were still coming. Fast. That hadn't been in the weather report.

I took a selfie. I have never taken many of those. I feel like you should earn it. Machu Picchu? Nah. The Taj Mahal? Hard pass. The day after your divorce? Getting closer. Mountains though. Now, there was a time to see your own face, no matter how much it might distort the scenery. *Click!*

I wrote a poem and left it in the battered metal box underneath four massive stones. I rubbed the geological survey marker, downed two power bars and a bottle of water, then sat, my legs dangling, my body facing the pass. The road below was gridlocked—an incongruous image contrasting the magnanimity of the universe's best paintbrush strokes with the short-sightedness of man. Another flash lanced toward the scene, an insistent reminder that could no longer be ignored. Menace hung thick on the breeze. It was time to get down.

At first, it was easy. I followed the simplest route, the path of least resistance. The guide had said to go counterclockwise when descending. My legs had that hollow, tremulous feeling that you get from high levels of adrenaline and moderate fatigue. I knew I had to get through the difficult parts quickly before the shakes set in. I made my way down the increasingly steep faces, sometimes spinning to face the mountain as necessary.

Rather than becoming broader and easier to navigate, the reverse occurred. The gaps were getting more and more difficult by the minute. I had a tickle at the back of my head; a cautious whisper telling me to swallow my pride and turn back. I ignored it.

I reached a narrow ledge. The middle was cleaved, with a narrow gap leading down to another, broader ledge below. I looked upwards and realized that I couldn't safely ascend. To my left was a giant boulder protruding out into space. To my right, a massive rockfall, loose to the touch. There was only one way out. I spun my pack around to my chest and sidled my hips down into the narrow inlet.

Gently now.

Adrenaline coursed through my veins. My body had finally woken up to how much danger I was in. I kept gently sliding down the crack. Each step was carefully planted, tested, then retested. I slid between handholds, my back pressed against the rock face.

Down I went. Ten feet. Twenty feet. Thirty... And all of a sudden, as much as rocks can be sudden, the crack corkscrewed downwards.

My legs shook under the strain. I could see that the rock ended, a fact that I hadn't been able to see from above. There was nothing but air, no handholds, just inverted stone.

Below was a narrow ledge, about three feet wide. I looked upward. I knew I didn't have the strength to get back up. I also knew, with startling clarity, that I couldn't wait long enough for a helicopter to arrive. I was cliffed out, exhausted, and caught between a rock and a hard place.

Another flash of light darted across the rock face. The sharp report of thunder quickly followed.

So this was it, eh?

I looked up to the sky and... said nothing. If there was a God, I was going to punch him squarely in the face as soon as I could manage. That motherfucker was going to answer to *me*. And I still had those questions. I was too angry to see that my attitude on the matter was a form of faith. I had no idea that my hatred was, in itself, a prayer.

Soon enough, my shaking legs began to slip and shimmy downward. I knew there was no more time to wait when my feet butted up against the edge.

The ledge below looked impossibly small. It was jagged, narrow, and ran horizontally along the mountain. There was no telling how far the drop was. From my vantage point, it was a perilous distance, one that only a movie star would survive. It could have been miles just as easily as a few inches. It was, most likely, three feet or so. Below it were countless thousands of feet... of air. Certain death. I could feel my hands starting to sweat, the murky, churning malaise that pours from your palms at the most inopportune times. But this wasn't a Homecoming Dance. This was a mountain that I had to get off, and these hands were the only things keeping me from taking the fast way down.

I have to jump.

I did. I had practiced it in my mind a thousand times, but nothing can prepare you for free fall. A single heartbeat stretched into years. Eternity compressed into a single second. I thought of my life in terms of one general idea: longing. It was pervasive, everything in a brief flash, a general understanding that might have been my final thought...

My legs hit the ledge and buckled. Backward. I had planned that. If I was going to lose my balance, it would be toward the relative safety of the wall. I leaned back to the waiting arms—and ricocheted. Hard. My knees were still half-bent, so my weight fully hit the stone. I was repelled forward, toward the maw...

Something might have intervened. There was a brief flash. The clouds, very close now, rippled with heat lightning. The boom was close enough to rattle my frame.

Without any independent thought, my legs shot out beneath me, my hip towards the crook of the wall behind. As the thunder rippled across the rock face, my ankles shot out over the expanse. I sat for a few breaths before I realized that I was still alive.

There was no time to revel. The wind was unrelenting now. Dark clouds stared deeply into my eyes, pulsing with rage, rushing toward my narrow perch. Raindrops began to gently alight on the rock. My breath caught and the moment stretched again.

There was an extension in the fabric of time and space, a forced inhale of gravity and reality. I saw my feet the same as I did as a child, dangling over a dock, watching a bobber slowly float towards the middle of the lake. I heard the giggle of the birds, the sharp exultations of the fish below the water, and the gentle assurance of every pine needle. The water of the lake merged with my body, flowing through the atmospheric channel as if... pushed—

More lightning. The noise of the thunder seemed strong enough to crack bone. I had to move. But there was nowhere to go...

The ledge ended abruptly, and I didn't have the strength to climb hundreds, or even thousands, of feet down. Nothing was going to save me in time. There was nothing I could do but wait for the end. Words tore from my lips.

"I FUCKING TRIED, YOU MONSTROUS ASSHOLE! I TRIED!! AND FOR WHA—"

Lightning. Thunder. Electricity coursed through the air. My hair stood up straight, pushing my thin ball cap away from my scalp and off into the abyss. I crouched in a ball and screamed.

It took a few moments to see the ray of light. It wasn't on me. It was shining through a hole in the clouds miles away, casting light on a random patch of land dozens of miles away. But its rapid appearance drew my eyes, pulling my attention from my impending doom, across the rock face...

Is that...?

The ledge to my left was less blocked than I had originally supposed. What seemed like a massive boulder was actually two. And there was a large crack between them.

I was up in a flash. It was a tight squeeze. My backpack dragged and caught, pulling backwards as I desperately surged forward.

Then I was through. The ledge broadened and widened, headed toward a gradually sloping set of stone terraces. They weren't just navigable. They were regular. After a few more paces, another ray of sunlight shot through the rapidly increasing rain drops. I looked up.

And then I saw the trail.

I was soaked to the bone when I made it to the parking lot. Despite the deluge of rain and sleet, and the intermittent pounding of thunder, there were still a few cars in the parking lot. The shuttles, however, had long since departed. I ran through the aisles on rubbery legs, sliding between the spots. All of the cars were empty.

That seemed impossible. There were too many of them. I checked my phone. It was dead.

I did the only sensible thing. I walked to the nearest pole, crumpled against it, and buried my head in my hands. The rain fell.

Self-pity, grief, and despair cascaded through me in waves, crashing through the high walls I had been hiding behind. I understood that I had been spared. Saved. But I didn't understand the meaning behind it. Why rescue someone from a house fire just to drown them in the pool? I felt the water seep ever deeper into my thin, polyester clothing. Then I heard the sound of approaching tires.

I looked up to an impossible sight. A brand-new Chevy Camaro, bright red and gleaming in the bleak twilight, had pulled over just feet away. The tires rapidly slowed, spitting water.

I shook my head, willing myself back to sanity. But the car was still there. The window rolled down and a middle-aged man with a crew cut poked his head out.

"I saw you running. You need a ride, buddy?"

"Thank you," I whispered.

I shook my head affirmatively, moved quickly toward the passenger-side door, and guiltily squirmed into the pristinely clean seat. My hands shook as he drove. I told the man my story, to which he sharply whistled.

"You must be damn good at prayin', son!" he exclaimed.

I'd never thought about it that way.

16

MANCORA

Blackness.

My hands trembled but stayed glued to the thin, sterile sheets below. I couldn't lift them. I could barely roll my head to the right... My blood felt thick... My toes could wiggle but my legs... Too heavy to move... There was an insistence... What was that? What the hell was going on?

A hand gently yet firmly caressed the bottom of my chin, pulling it towards the edge of the bed. A stout brown woman was perched on a stool. She was middle-aged, her face deeply creased with laugh and worry lines. Her black hair was tied in a pert knot behind her head. Narrow silver loops hung from her ears. She was insistently waving a spoon in front of my lips. Here came the airplane, ready or not. Flashes of memory shot through a ragged, torn mind...

A pool of vomit. Six inches high. I was prone, face down, on a paper-thin mattress. People were yelling in several languages. The stench was enough to blind. I couldn't move...

Blackness.

***

Something was dripping down my neck, but I couldn't raise my arms to wipe it away. I had no recollection of getting out of bed. I was being dragged, multiple hands around my waist, chest, and legs. My ankles pulled and caught on the sand. My body was roughly tossed into the seat of a rickshaw. The doors slammed, once, twice... The wheels spun furiously...

***

Hands gripped, pushing me down. Every muscle and fiber fought furiously. Voices shouted in Spanish. I could make out various curses and the word 'gringo' through the haze. Pressure came from four points on my chest. My eyes flew open, followed by a muffled scream. A hand was over my mouth. A woman was on my chest, knees pressed into my shoulders. There was a pinch in my arm...

***

Blackness.

There was no telling how long I'd been drifting. The spoon rested on the woman's lap, and she was clapping her hands. My unfiltered eyes focused. A stomach disconnected from my frame rumbled with a deep and desperate longing. The tremor shook my entire body, sending spasms of pain through my abdomen. The woman quickly began spoon feeding me. It was soup, salty and tangy. It was the single best thing that I have ever tasted. She patiently pushed bit after bit into my mouth, occasionally wiping my chin.

One dream faded as the wisps of another returned. This one was familiar. I'd had it for weeks as I'd run, run, run... Snatches of a life I'd left behind, the rerun airing over and over...

Blackness.

***

I hadn't seen her coming. The run came down over the crest of the largest hill in the distance, then angled sharply back in toward the resort. She'd cut through the trees. With zero hesitation, her skis were off and she was running through the snow. She unzipped my jacket and put her hands around my waist in a tight squeeze, burying her head into my chest. Her questions came rapid-fire.

"Are you okay? What happened? Your head... What is wrong with your ear..."

I tried to answer a few times but then gave in. The relief was a drug that coated every vein. My heart eased into itself. Despite the chaos behind, she was in front of me. That was all I needed.

"YOU broke that window?? How is your hand... Where are you staying... Are they going to let you keep working?"

I stopped listening and laid my head against her neck. Her heartbeat was an anxious twitter, pulsing against the softest, sweetest skin. My hands trembled, either from withdrawal or longing. It was always hard to tell which.

"...are you listening to me?"

Yes, dear. Yes, I am.

I told her everything. From the hot tub to Human Resources. She looked down at the ground and saw the pint laying there. A wash of shame crept up from my ankles. I looked down, and she mirrored the movement. I lit a cigarette and turned so that she couldn't see the tears in my eyes.

"I love you," I blurted out. I couldn't hold it in anymore. "You're the only reason I'm still here..."

"Well," she said, coolly. "Maybe you shouldn't be." Then she laughed, took the cigarette from my hand, and took a long drag. I could feel her eyes on the side

of my head. She had a coolly appraising quality to her at times. Her father had died when she was young. Her eyes told a story of a girl who had grown old a little too soon. "I guess there are worse things."

The tears started to flow, unbidden, down the sides of my face. I kept my expression completely rigid, barely bothering to breathe. This was the dam, overflowed; the reactor, melting down. Time passed. The next thing I remembered, she was back inside my jacket, my ribcage quaking from the force of her arms. She was trying to squeeze directly into my heart. If I had budged, I would've boiled into the snow and straight into the core of the Earth. Her breath came up in hot clouds of vapor under my chin.

"You're not nearly as bad as you think, Sam," she said. I wanted to believe her. I desperately needed to hold onto the hope that this hadn't all been for nothing. I needed to say something, to show her strength, kindness, and protection. Nothing came out. Instead, I kissed the top of her head.

When she pulled away, I lit another cigarette. She was eyeing me up and down, gently this time. I gave her the best smile a man with frozen tears caking his cheeks can give. The sun was high above our heads. Her bright red hair caught a slight gust and streaked across her face. She gently pushed it to the side and looked down the mountain. The run below us was empty, undulating mounds softly beckoning.

"You wanna race?" I asked her. She smiled and fumbled on the ground for her helmet.

"Last one down buys the first round..." She started to say.

"Umm... about that..."

"I heard. At my place."

I got my gear together faster than Shaun White in front of an avalanche. She was already moving swiftly downward as I got my edge in and started to move. I could tell she was taking it easy. She had watched me fall so many times... patiently laughing and encouraging me as I learned. What she didn't know was that I had been practicing.

We picked up speed. Her skis were neat and tight, expertly moving back and forth. I caught myself staring. I needed to focus. I realized that I had to win. Not for any of the fringe benefits, either. There was something desperate about it. A primal urge to prove dominance and secure... something. I couldn't lose her. If I did, I had nothing. If I did...

...I was nothing.

I could sense her shock when I came screaming around her. My second-hand board shouldn't have been able to move that fast. There was a patch of duct tape holding one of the bindings together. It rattled, buckled, and flapped. I was in my flow. The wind and I were one. I was a hot knife cutting through the frigid air. My soul, life, and purpose were one and the same—

And with a muted crack, my board snapped. I went tumbling, my gear and I reduced to a yard sale on the pristinely white powder beneath. She looked back once, shook her head, and disappeared around the bend.

***

Blackness.

A hand was firmly grabbing my foot. More voices in Spanish. The hand became more insistent. I opened my eyes. A man in a white lab coat stood at the foot of the bed. Two women were also there, arms crossed, staring at my exposed chest. I tried to move my arms and couldn't. They had been tied to the bed. I could feel things inside of them... IVs. Two of them. Ah, shit. I said something eloquent, a verbose elucidation of my thoughts:

"...fuuuck?"

More Spanish. I tried to roll my head, my eyes and nostrils flaring. Spent sweat had glued my remaining whatever I was wearing to my skin. I was cold, despite the raging inferno coming from the windows. I stared at the foreign faces in front of me. For the first time, I became scared of death. I thought of what I had missed; all of the love that I had yet to find. Oddly enough, I thought of calling my brother.

The doctor became frustrated and stormed out of the room. Seconds later, he returned with the nurse who had been spoon-feeding me at night. She was the only one who spoke English and, even then, not very well. Bits and fragments emerged. All I really understood was the word "*muerte*." Death. Well then. The doctor held up his thumb and forefinger, close together. The woman repeated the rapid-fire Spanglish that I still couldn't process. "*Muerte*" was repeated. I finally got the gist. The doctor then held up a syringe and I nodded. It went into one of the IVs.

Blackness.

***

Blackness.

Consciousness returned slowly. When it did, there was an urgency. One of the IVs had been removed, leaving me with one in my left arm, attached to a moveable pole. Stricken, wobbling, and dazed, I rolled off of the thin mattress and staggered to the bathroom.

Blood came out of me in violent pulses. Looking down was a recipe for vomiting, so I sat, eyes peeled, praying for mercy. Loud pounding came from the ill-fitting door. I slowly drew in the IV, cleaned myself the best I could, and staggered back to my narrow room. As I did, I flashed a giant, solitary finger toward the waiting room.

Still got it.

Occasionally there would be another patient in the bed next to me. As I drifted in and out of consciousness, I would return to see varying numbers of cockroaches scurrying across the ceiling. Waiting, it seemed. I could usually feel something thick and sticky making its way down my leg. As had become the norm, memories returned.

Machu Picchu. Standing atop the mountain, arms spread wide, lost in the bright sunlight...

An Irish bar in Cusco. Dancing on the tables with the Israeli girls...

Running barefoot through the slums of Lima, a can of spray paint in my hand...

Sirens. Drinking. Partying. Drugs. Street food. Fancy shoes...

A woman dressed only in a thin sheet, turning slowly on top of a crumbling rooftop...

I'd been a pale, fast-walking tornado, consuming the country and culture at a reckless pace. At some point, I had hopped on a *colectivo*, a dented white van with no markings, filled with all shapes and sizes of Peruvians. The driver grinned at the open beer in my hand and peeled off onto the highway.

I'd known I was headed North. The destination didn't matter. It turned out to be Mancora, a party town. The first hostel I passed had a bar and people playing volleyball in the pool. It was a frat party disguised as a bunk house. I had wanted to fit in so badly that I had forgotten who I was. I was the black wolf masquerading as a fluffy white sheep, desperate not to show the bleeding wounds on my underbelly.

The stress of lying to one and all had led to an intense need to medicate. And medicate I did, becoming ever more belligerent as the night passed. Eventually, I had gone outside and made some very bad decisions. Men had followed me inside. I'd thought nothing of it. I was invincible. The American. Brash, loud, and unaffected by the proverbial bullshit. I was ripe for the picking…

Blackness.

***

Blackness.

I tossed and turned on the bed, growing more restless with each passing hour. The older woman had disappeared, replaced by a woman of startling beauty. She was dressed in bright purple scrubs and wore dark-rimmed glasses that were much larger than her narrow face. Kindness radiated from her, an aura of compassion that dominated the room.

There was no telling how long she had been sitting there when I awoke, or if I had been sleeping at all. She held a bag in her hands. It was filled to the brim with pastries and rolls. She pulled one out and waved it in front of my face. It smelled of sugar and cinnamon. I tried to lift my head, failed, and fell back. She gently *tsked* and slid the chair closer. Her body leaned across the sweat-soaked sheets as she propped my head up, then held the pastry close to my mouth. I took a bite. Then another. The effort of chewing was exhausting. Each mouthful burned, a torrent of blazing fire that came in stark contrast to the symphony of taste on my tongue. I was a baby, cradled in the arms of an angel. When I consumed the bag, the woman sat back and crossed her hands over her lap.

Blackness.

***

I awoke again, gently this time. Something rested against my inner thighs... another bag of pastries. A container of soup sat on the bedside table, alongside a cell phone that looked suspiciously like mine. I looked down at my legs and found that my pants had been removed, replaced with a hospital gown.

I could feel a twinkle of strength. I found that I could pull backward... Slowly, I rose to a seated position. With frenzied motions, I devoured everything in the bag, then grabbed the container of soup and drank it straight. Noodles flopped and fell across my chest. Whatever. I had long since lost any sense of dignity. A thought crept into my mind.

"*Muerte.*"

I had to find out what was happening.

Before I had time to think of the consequences, I was out of bed. With one hand on the wall, the other desperately gripping the IV stand, I crept across the room. I hesitated at the first door, then burst through and made my way to the front entrance. Loud yelling and protestations followed me, but I made it down the narrow, tilted stairs.

The street was unpaved, just ungroomed sand and dirt mixed with gravel. With my pale white ass prominently displayed to anyone who bothered to look and the IV stand haphazardly leaning against my shoulder, I powered on my phone. I hadn't turned it on in a week but, miracles abound, it had a little juice. I could feel the eyes glued to me and hear the rapidly approaching sound of footsteps. My fingers rapidly typed, and I connected to the first Wi-Fi signal I could get.

Another miracle, there was an unsecured hotspot available. I connected, pulled up social media, and rattled off a quick status report. I hit send but something tickled, and it wasn't the hand that suddenly gripped my shoulder. On a whim, I reopened the post and added the name of the clinic and a location. It seemed like the right thing to do. Then I was rudely escorted back to my bed.

The next day, one of the male orderlies woke me up and gestured for me to get up. This took a while. Strength was returning, but I could feel sharp pains in my intestines. My kidneys and liver felt as if they were filled with small stones. The man's expression softened as I grimaced, and he began to help me stagger to the door.

We shuffled past the staring eyes in the foyer, and somehow managed to finagle me and my IV into the rickshaw he had arranged for. My stunt the day before had made them worried that I would leave without paying. As a result, we were on a field trip to the ATM. The bank had Wi-Fi though, and my escort had a charger. I logged into social media again. My post had generated some interest.

Hundreds of comments and messages populated every outlet I had. 'She' had even sent me a message. One of my buddies from Argentina was adamantly asking where I was. He had been trying to get ahold of the clinic for days. I had spelled it wrong. When we returned, they had connected to my adamant translator. Thus, after eight days, I was finally told what had happened.

I had been poisoned. Somewhere in that first night they had taken blood samples and rushed them to another town. I also had an ulcer, a bad case of salmonella, a criminal amount of alcohol in my system and, oh yeah, *poison*.

The assholes that had come into the bar had slipped something into my drink that was intended to be lethal. The antibiotics that they were pumping into my system weren't designed to counteract anything like that. I had survived solely off of my "innate abilities." I didn't think that was correct, but I nodded and played along. The stress and heat of the day had drained what little strength I had left. I thanked my friend and promised to name my firstborn after him, then slipped...

I woke in the middle of the night to an empty room—wait, no, not empty. The nurse in the purple scrubs was back, sitting on a stool in the darkness. A thin light permeated the air, slitting through the cracked curtain, narrowly highlighting a warm smile. A spoon appeared at my mouth. Words poured out. Profuse utterances of gratitude, atonement, and pleading for an end to the pain...

The woman gently *tsked* and pushed the spoon into my mouth. Around bites, I tried to tell her that I adored her, that I would love her endlessly till the sun winked out in the sky... More soup. I could hear her softly laughing. Her eyes glimmered. I tried to reach out for her then, to touch the grace and beauty that poured from her being. My hand touched nothing but air. More soup. Time abbreviated again.

When I returned to full consciousness, she was gone. I reached down and found another bag of pastries between my legs. The night outside was silent and warm.

I was released two days later. My insides were bruised and battered, my tenuous grip on self-confidence utterly shattered. I was a broken husk of a human, staggering out of the clinic with my tail between my legs. I sheepishly turned to the woman at the front desk, tugging at her sleeve. I hadn't seen her before. She spoke some English.

"Will you thank the other woman for me?" I managed, meekly.

"*Que?*" the woman replied. She was baffled and looked at me with concern.

"The young woman with the soup and pastries? The one who was taking care of me? *Lo entiendes?*"

"Young woman?" she replied, growing more confused. "No hay mujeres jovenes aqui." Her response was flat, final.

Now I was confused. I thanked her and slowly made my way towards the light. The sun shone impossibly bright outside. A searing heat blared through the crack of the door.

At the foot of the stairs, the young woman in the purple scrubs was stepping into a *colectivo*. Her eyes were bright and her smile was wide. Something shone from her... indescribable. I tried to open the door and couldn't. That side was locked. The young woman quickly raised a hand and waved. She darted through the door and closed it behind her. The van was already slowly rolling through the loose sand and dirt.

I tried to hurry and failed. When I made it to the bottom of the stairs, sweating profusely, I could still see the battered white van fading in the distance. I couldn't be sure, but I thought I could see a hand, faintly waving in the back row. I looked up to the sun and sighed. I took one step, then another, and slowly made my way back to the hostel to pick up my things.

17

CREEDE

I gripped the front of the dash as she pulled onto the side of the road. Not the 'good' side of the road, mind you. The other one, next to the opposing lane. I could hear the engine of the small truck redlining.

Terror had been driving like she usually did, foot to the floor, holding the wheel with her wrists while unscrewing another mini bottle, all while passing a car that was passing another car. This time, however, it was on a banked, blind corner. Horns blared from everywhere.

For the thousandth time since I met her, I rued my suspended license. Usually, it wasn't a concern. I could drink as much as I wanted in the passenger seat, guilt-free. It worked for me, kind of. Until she did shit like this. I took a bottle out of the cup holder, took a swig, then gripped it tightly.

I wasn't going to spill my beer for this shit.

We hit a small bump and the cab shook violently from side to side. I looked over at the speedometer. It read a steady 120 mph. That was the limit of how far up it went. You could get away with that kind of speed in those parts. There was just too much road and not enough money to pay the cops. And the ones that you did see were too busy getting paid off by the cartels to notice one small Chevy with a faded paint job flying past. Horns blared. We were passing everyone, she just had to—

The hole appeared and she hit it expertly. I had to hand it to her. For all the crazy shit like this that she pulled, she missed her calling as a race car driver. The truck somehow managed to accelerate, moving swiftly into the correct lane on the freeway. She banked into a turn, then another, flying up the narrow highway. I finished my beer, then opened two more and handed one to her. She downed half the bottle in one chug, belched, then turned up the music. Her face crumpled in a frown. She was upset about something.

It was probably the fact that we were on our way to get her an abortion. Or maybe it was something about work—no. It was definitely the abortion.

We both worked at a small-town bar, nestled in the mountains of Southern Colorado. The closest place to get one of these procedures was five hours away. Terror was my best friend. I couldn't let her go alone. Plus, I had a thing for nurses.

The baby wasn't mine. She had shown up for the season already knocked up. We had been out drinking for the tenth consecutive day. There was a saloon in town that stayed open as long as we were spending money. There was nothing else to do, so we took the lemons we had and made margaritas. I remember knocking back a shot of Fireball, everyone in the bar joining in, when Terror had silently appeared at my elbow. She was pissed.

Her name wasn't really Terror, but it might as well have been. She was a massive human, half-Samoan, with a massive head and broad shoulders. She stood at least six feet, but she also had a nimble grace. This was most likely from a life spent behind a bar and behind bars, where space comes at a premium. She could *move* when necessary.

I found this out on more than a few nights when she crawled into my bed, pushed anyone who was already in it off to the side, and furiously cuddled me. I was usually laughing too hard to say no.

Terror constantly gave off the impression that she wanted to crack your neck between her enormous tits. She was loud, passionate, abrasive, and utterly unapologetic. So when she appeared the way she did that night, wringing her hands and furtively looking at the ground, a blind man could have sensed that something was awry.

After a brief pause, she reached around me, brusquely dragging her immense gazoombas across my back and arm, grabbed the bottle of whiskey I had bought, and took a deep pull. Then she spun me around, put both of her hands on my shoulders, and looked me straight in the eyes.

"I'm pregnant," she said.

Her eyes were limned with red; the fringes of her eye sockets more sunken than normal. She had been crying. I should also mention, Terror was an absolute asshole at all times. She had no tact or accountability, and never considered the repercussions of her behavior. I immediately tried to do the math. She had crawled in my bed nine nights ago... or was it ten...

Good God. Did we have sex?

Luckily, she laughed. "Oh no, dumbass. It's not yours. Some guy in Texas. Or maybe Oklahoma."

Sweet heavenly father of all that is holy, thank you. I am sorry for my sins. Please forgive me. Thank you. I will pray more, I promise. Thank you, thank you, thank you...

I returned her stare for a few seconds. Then I said something warm and comforting, like: "Well, shit!"

I certainly have my moments.

My support and kindness had no effect. She began tearing her way through the bottle so fast that I grabbed it from her. This was a daunting thing to do. Getting in between a bear and her cub is never a good idea. But she didn't try to eat my face or tear my arms off. Instead, she did something I hadn't seen her do. She became very afraid.

I had only known this woman for a month at this point. We were the two talented bartenders in a very small town. This equated to a high social status that we took full advantage of. The restaurant was a legendary place. I worked the upstairs, she worked the lower level. Between us, we cranked out enough drinks to sate the hordes of Texan tourists that flocked there in the summer. We made serious dough.

We had become fixtures at the saloon, waddling over after we had finished mopping, always greeted with cheers and warm smiles. And we had quickly become inseparable. It was an arrangement of convenience, a meeting of star-crossed misanthropes ravenous for companionship. We shared the immutable bond of the completely self-reliant. But here was something real, a life-changing moment that she couldn't face on her own.

There was no option but to find a place to get the procedure. Politics and morality aside, we both knew that with the amount of alcohol she had poured into her body over the past few months, there was absolutely no way that a healthy child was going to come out of her. We would fly to Europe if we had to.

There was also the fact that she was on the run from something. She'd kept it close to the chest, but it was obvious that she was lying low. And having a child while you're trying to stay five steps ahead of the Marshalls is just a bad strategy any way that you slice it. I handed the bartender a fifty, took the bottle, and we went to the corner of the room to start Googling instructions.

A week had passed since then. She had waffled once, at which point I had to take the cocktail out of her hand and explain to her, in vivid detail, what fetal alcohol syndrome was. It was then that she revealed that she already had a child, and that she had given birth to that child in prison... I plied her for details but received none. She had completely shut down.

Well, shit.

I was already in. There was no running now. Even if I had tried, where the hell could I go? I knew how fast she drove. She'd track me down, hand me a beer, then bear hug me on the side of the road until I wasn't mad anymore. For all her faults, Terror had a heart of gold. And that heart was breaking for what she had to do. I kept her between the lines, made sure we had the days off that we needed, and ushered her toward the finish line. A line we were now approaching at a speed that would kill us on impact.

"Hey, Terror?" I said, reaching over to turn down the stereo. It took a serious effort to keep my voice level. I could feel the dashboard beneath my hand, the engine straining and groaning... "Let's make it there alive, eh? Terror. TERROR!"

Her eyes remained fixed on the road ahead, but I could see some of the tension start to drain away. The truck began to slow. Groaning. Grinding. The barren landscape to the side of the highway remained unchanged. The desert gave the impression of finality, infinity...

I knew this wasn't 'it.' Somewhere, there was a place for me. Out there... I reached over and put a hand on her shoulder. Her façade was cracking, the tough demeanor rupturing, fractures splitting to the heartwood. She drained the rest of her bottle and patted my hand.

"It's gonna be alright, Terror," I said.

"I know, muffin."

...

Muffin?

...

Ah.

I did what I did best, ignoring reality and creating my own. I looked down at my feet and counted the bottles. There were plenty left. I busied myself picking out a new playlist. The road hammered away, the truck continued to whine, albeit less intensely, and the broad expanse flashed past. Tumbleweeds rolled across the tar-lined pavement until they were crushed underneath our tires.

My hand still hovered above the surface of the dash. I cast furtive glances at her. I wasn't in love, not even close. I was very fond of her, though. I hadn't had a friend like that before. Ride or die. Someone who would have your back, no matter what. And I felt the same.

Despite her size, she looked small then. We were just two kids, adrift in an extended childhood, drifting aimlessly across the Wild West. Outlaws, completely detached from the real world. We could have been abducted by aliens without batting an eye. I should have said something then, anything to ease her mind. Instead, I took another swig and stared out the window.

It only took two more stops at the liquor store to get us the rest of the way. When we pulled into the parking lot, Terror's fists clenched around the wheel, her white knuckles began to pop. As the engine died, wheezing with exhaustion, she leaned her chair back and cracked a mini-bottle. I started to speak, but she cut me off.

"I can do this."

I nodded and we crossed the parking lot. I put a hand on her broad back as we passed the picket line. Several protestors stepped briefly in the way, but immediately thought better of it.

When we approached the desk, the nurse at the front smiled and handed us a stack of forms. I ducked into one of the chairs and filled them out for her, occasionally asking her questions. I received terse, faraway responses. Then a pair of stout nurses popped into the room and called her name. She stood without a word and followed them through the double doors.

Hours passed. I caught a lot of meaningful looks from the women behind the counter. Terror had been adamant that the child wasn't mine. I couldn't bring myself to rise to the occasion. In that setting, primal desires took a backseat to vicious realities.

Dozens of terrified women surrounded me, all huddled in cloaks of grief and self-loathing. This was a stark reminder that everything can change in an instant, that our entire trajectory can be altered by one broken condom or poor decision. For the first time, I considered a different way of life. In the background, the chants of the protestors were barely muffled by the blaring TVs and air conditioning. I kept my eyes peeled on the doorway, just in case.

Hours later, Terror emerged. She was staggering, a shredded and shattered husk of the human that had passed through earlier that morning. I rushed to her side and slid under her armpit. The two nurses stood in the hallway, looking thoroughly exhausted. We left by the back door.

Terror tried to get in the driver's seat, but I refused. Something had shifted in that clinic. It was time to take the wheel for a while. I drove for a few hours, then found us a hotel. The town was nameless; a bar, gas station, and the room I had rented were the only evidence of human habitation.

I checked in, then went to collect my friend. She barely made it through the door. With one giant step forward, she collapsed on the bed. A single, brazen spear of daylight came through the drawn curtains. Terror's mask had fallen, her mystique and strength completely stripped away. She was snoring within seconds. I spent the rest of the afternoon on one arm, gently brushing her coarse hair away from her face.

Somewhere around dinnertime, she awoke. Her eyes blinked once, twice... A grimace twisted across her mouth.

"Is there a bar nearby?"

***

Dust was everything and everywhere. We lived on the sand, rootless and migratory. It was a transitory existence spent at free campsites and barren expanses of BLM land. We were as wild and unchained as the scenery. Jobs and money came and went without rhyme or reason. Our only contact with humanity was a loose assembly of malcontents and meth heads, most of whom stayed as far away from us as possible.

Battering winds stirred up the dust and sent it hurtling toward my face. There was no possibility of warmth. A strict fire ban was in effect. Thick trails of smoke wafted through the sage and scrub pine, remnants of a wildfire somewhere nearby. I lifted my last beer and drained it, then lit a cigarette. I was outside. Terror was napping in the tent.

We were not getting along.

I had been fired from the bar in Colorado. The owner had seen himself in me, and vice versa. It had been destined to boil over from the moment I arrived. Honestly, I was surprised that I had lasted as long as I did.

After picking up my last check, I went to the saloon down the street and waited. It didn't take long to hear the yelling. As Terror stormed across the weathered floors into the dark gloom that I sat in, she raised her arms and hooted. I heaved a sigh of relief and finished my beer. I lit two cigarettes and handed her one. Two hours later, we were on the road.

For the next two months we traipsed along the west coast, doing odd jobs and dropping in on friends. The money had run out in Bend. There were countless free places to camp in the area, so we'd pitched a tent and both gotten jobs. But without the framework of the bar and the insulating presence of all of the other friends we had made, Terror had begun to grate on me. Fiercely. What was once a constant back-and-forth had first devolved to bickering, then to open warfare.

The stress mounted by the day. It was only a matter of time, now.

With the dust, smoke, and sand whipping my face, I stared at the tent. I'd had enough. There were too many lies. A mountain of half-truths lay between us like an open laptop showing last night's surveillance footage. I couldn't take the stress that emanated from her, and I knew she felt the same. I had booked a ticket up to Portland the night before. I was just waiting for her to sober up to break the news.

It didn't go over well. The fight was short and loud. Shortly after, we found ourselves in the narrow cab, violently rocking back and forth as she tore down the loose dirt roads. We had almost made it to civilization before we passed a sheriff, cleverly tucked away behind a road sign. He caught up to us quickly, the bright blue and red lights on top of his squad car blazing in the dim morning light. She pulled over and began to wring her hands. Words tumbled out in fits and starts.

"I've been running for a while. I did my time. But they wanted so much..." she began.

"So much wh—"

"Money. I never showed up for parole. When they let me out..." Her arms trembled as she spoke. Terror had crept into her voice, a stark contrast to the effect that she exuded. The sheriff was at the window now, gently tapping. She rolled down the window and put up one finger.

"Just a moment, officer. Then I will come quietly."

To my amazement, the officer put up both hands and complied.

From somewhere behind her seat, she pulled out two 4Lokos. Repugnant stuff, each the equivalent of a six-pack and a pot of coffee in one can. They were good for one thing: getting absolutely annihilated. Fast. She cracked one, chugged the entire thing, then snapped her fingers. I didn't move, so she violently reached down and snatched the pack of cigarettes from my lap. Then she paused, sighed, lit two cigarettes at once, and handed me one.

"I'm sorry, muffin. I won't be able to take you to the train station. I have to go away for a while."

My eloquence and tact are bottomless. I am a paragon of suavity; a stoic fortress of strength and compassion.

"Well... shit," I said.

"That's all you've got to say?" She asked. Her eyes would have melted the hardest of hearts. They were bottomless pits of grief, moist as a puppy's, wide as a child seeing their first big-screen movie. I softened.

"You should have told me this months ago."

She shrugged, deflated. I didn't love her, and she knew it. And I had never signed on to be a fugitive. I had other crosses to die on. Suddenly, she straightened. Something primal reawakened within her. A fraction of the old swagger returned to her frame.

"You're right. I'm sorry," she mumbled.

"I forgave you a long time ago, Terror."

She smiled at that. Her cigarette had burned to the nub, so I lit another one and handed it to her. She took her time with the second can. The sheriff had returned to the window, beckoning. She took the keys from the ignition and handed them over. The man was completely baffled.

"Just another minute, officer. I'm coming."

And with that, she finished the can, took another drag, then leaned across the seat and planted a fat kiss on my cheek. Her thick, wet lips lingered on my unshaved stubble. It was just a moment, an illusory snatch of time, yet it was ample time for something to pass between us—an understanding of sorts.

She crumpled the can, slowly rolled out of the driver's seat, and walked to the officer. The truck whined and shimmied, seemingly... relieved. As she approached his vehicle, she put her hands forward and placed them on the hood. I let myself out of the passenger seat and watched as he cuffed her, then guided her into the back seat. I could not see through the tinted windows, but I was sure she was watching me through the bars. The officer tossed me the keys.

"She'll need some money for the commissary," the man said. He was smiling now. That collar must have been the highlight of his week. I was too stunned to speak, so I just nodded. The squad car started with a roar, then took off down the narrow road, bright red tail lights beaming through a thick dust cloud.

I stood and watched the massive plume gently settle. The whole world seemed silent, as if it was holding its breath. And as the last motes fell to the ground, she was gone.

18

MEDFORD

I awoke to a loud buzzing coming from somewhere between the sheets. Despite it being mid-morning, the room was pitch-black. The sun wouldn't rise for another hour or two.

Typically, my phone was easy to ignore, but that day something felt off. I hadn't been sleeping well. Anxiety dominated my innards, one that I couldn't explain. I searched and rooted around my girlfriend's sleeping body. She huffed once, dug deep under her side, and handed it to me. I answered the call with a terse grunt.

The voice on the other end was tense and full of alarm. It was a woman's voice that I couldn't place… Ah, my father's partner. I had missed her first words, so she repeated them.

"Something has happened," she said.

I snapped awake, dragging myself up against the pillows. Alarmed, my girlfriend shot up alongside. She'd been distant for some time, wrapped up in her own mind. Neither of us wanted to admit that it wasn't working. But this call was clearly beyond all of that. Her hands wrapped around my rigid body, clinging tightly. I sagged into her. I could feel her shaking… or was it me?

My father's partner launched into a long, detailed description. Understanding came in fits and starts. My father had cancer. Catastrophic. Stage 4. Everywhere. They had immediately operated, tearing holes in more places than anyone cared to describe. His voice box had been removed. He was alive. There wasn't much time.

These are the calls that we dread. For most, their entire lives are flipped like a coin flying through the air. I had no idea what I thought or how to feel. I wanted to jump out of bed and go for a run. But a blizzard had rudely dumped feet of snow everywhere in sight the day before. Running anywhere was impossible.

Alaska. How did I end up here?

I hated the place I lived. I hated everything. I was a miser, living in a town I couldn't escape from, in a nightmare life that pulled me further in as it pushed me further away. I was pale saltwater taffy, caught between the door and the frame. I had planned a vacation long ago, an attempt to get away from it all. Now this.

There wouldn't be any running from this.

I got to work checking flights. My girlfriend asked no questions, instead heading straight for the shower. I had long known that I was simply the financial engine that brought her where she wanted to go. The weight of my emotional baggage was mine to carry. There was another ding from my phone. The tickets were booked. A sense of finality began to set in.

My father was dying. I'd always thought that there was an infinite amount of time, that one day my anger would magically disappear. Something deep within longed for the possibility that we could reconnect... that I could finally get all the love and understanding that I deserved. With a grim finality, I knew it had always been a pipe dream.

A blow dryer angrily whined in the bathroom. Then she emerged, stark naked, and walked right past my outstretched hand to the wardrobe. When I told her about the flight, she asked me how long I would be gone, nodded, then dressed quickly and went to work. Confirmations were coming fast and furious that day. I lay in bed for another hour until it was my turn to get ready.

Work was a daze. I'd receded within long before; burned out to a shade of black that I couldn't recognize. My attitude had created another situation like Sol Duc. Yet again, I was the misunderstood misanthrope. The angry, vengeful pariah. There was nothing left to do but make drinks and keep my head down. After my shift ended, it was a long, quiet ride down to Anchorage. I checked my phone every twenty minutes, afraid that he would die ahead of schedule.

The flights were violent, jittery, and bumpy. One of the connections almost slid off the runway. When I arrived, shaken and exhausted, I found out that my mother had forgotten to pick me up. Instead, I took the train to the bus station and waited 'til my brother arrived. At least he was on time.

For the first time, he seemed grateful for my company. I had always been someone he could depend on. Now, this was something he indulged himself in. We were going to borrow my mother's car so that I could drive us down to Medford. Despite a rapidly growing sense of dread, I couldn't wait to get on the highway. I stood up straight, cracked jokes, and remembered how it felt to be fifteen.

We stopped only for fast food and cigarettes. Rain came in buckets, then sheets, then slowed to a persistent drizzle. My brother would later claim that I drove like a demon, passing cars and terrifying the entire I-5 corridor. But he had never driven a car in his life, so he didn't get to complain. I thought I drove fine. We made great time.

My hands began to shake when we pulled into the hospital parking lot. I hadn't seen my father in years, and we hadn't sat together for longer than a few hours since I was a teenager. It had always seemed like he was just as eager to get away from me as I was from him. What would we say? What *could* we say? Then I remembered that they had removed his voice box. There was no "we." I guess there never had been. I would just have to figure it out as I went.

The hospital was a blur of concerned faces. If I knew a damn thing about my father, the lack of vocal cords wouldn't have stopped him from flirting with every woman in the building. They all knew we were coming. There was even a nurse parked outside his room. This is a universally bad sign. It means that someone desperately needs constant vigilance. To him, it might be a matter of life and death. To me, it was a nuisance.

I was here to let him go. I needed to forge a path through the ravages of time, to find a way to forgive a monster. That necessitated a little privacy, thank you. Nothing ever goes perfectly, though. The nurse stayed where she was.

The man actually managed to stand up when we entered. It made sense. He had taught me to always dress up for a funeral and to never shake a man's hand while sitting down. He waved off the nurse. Dressed in a cotton gown, recently sponge-bathed, and with his hair done up in his customary slick-back, he could have been there for a routine colonoscopy. Aside from the gaping wounds, of course.

This was the first time that the three of us had stood in the same room for more than a decade. We all shuffled. If it hadn't been so awkward, it would have been hilarious to watch us all make the same nervous movements side to side.

None of us looked alike. Aside from our grins, our gaits, and the way that we moved our heads, strangers would be hard-pressed to link us in a crowd. But if you watched closely, the three of us made the same movements with our hands. The same curve of the left sides of our mouths. The same movement of index finger to the bridge of our glasses. Whether or not our mother had been lying to us all of these years, as our father believed, we mimicked each other perfectly.

The man's throat was grotesquely distended. Blues and purples dotted his neckline. I could tell there were other deformities hidden underneath the soft blue gown. Was this really the man who had thrown me around so many times? Who had run away from my life more times than I could count? Who had put a gun to my head and... Was this really the man who had terrorized so many of my dreams? It couldn't be.

He gave me his best rakish smile. A large percentage of it made it through his puffed, swollen face. It was for my brother. We both knew that. I have never hidden my trauma. It lives on my sleeve; a giant bag that has broken my shoulders with time and repeated wear. But I have always been able to work through it, however slowly. My brother is different, impossibly soft and brittle. Gentle and meek, a lamb thrown headfirst into a world of snarling wolves. I matched my father's grin and tried my best to make the jokes I knew he would make. The burden would fall on me now. My brother's face had gone a deathly shade of pale.

Luckily, the nurse chose that moment to check on us. She didn't pay any mind when the old man waved at her to scram. I knew that she had rehearsed it with him before we had arrived.

He insisted on taking a picture. It had been the same throughout our lives. He would pop in, spend a few hours, take a photo, then *poof!* Gone. Years would pass, the photos stuffed in a box somewhere in the closet. When we were young, we had stayed up late, eager to see him again, crawling up the walls with excitement as he was on his way. We had quickly reached an age where we stopped waiting.

I could tell that we had a very short window. He was undoubtedly on a lot of painkillers, and was probably taking a short break to be coherent for us. We wasted no time. As soon as the flash of the camera receded, he waved my brother away and laid back down on the bed. As he did, he became tangled in the cords of his... shit-bag. There was another one too... I jumped over and untangled him. Everything flopped out—dick, shit, piss... the works. The brown bag flopped to the side as the yellow bag started to slide...

I caught it just before it fell. Some liquid seeped out of the gasket. I wiped it on the edge of the bed. There I was, yet again, caught holding the bag. But there was something I knew well by then. Sometimes you just have to ignore the score and play the damn game. He started to look down in shame...

"Not so bad, Dad," I said, flashing a grin. Rakish. Tilted.

There it was. His favorite phrase. I remembered what it meant to him.

Tears sprung to his eyes. I watched the monster wilt, reduced by the ravages of time to a shucked shell, his organs ruptured, severed, and split. He was involuntarily thrown back into his infancy, a mewling babe that needed his waste disposed of. Just like we all were. And, if we're lucky, will be again.

Suddenly, he looked a hell of a lot more human.

I remembered the kitchen floor where he had wept in my arms. I remembered the beach house. That damn chair... I didn't know what the words meant yet, but my intentions were simple: grace, forgiveness, and understanding. I knew him better than he thought. I had seen him in the mirror more times than I cared to admit. I looked at him with eyes I had been preparing for days. He couldn't meet them.

Instead, he pulled a whiteboard out from under his pillow. It had pens attached. His little hands shook as he scribbled. I could see the rips and slashes across his arms as the gown receded. It took him a while to get the board turned around.

"Who's the girl?" it said.

I told him. Words came out in an unbidden flow, a deluge of water let free from behind a dam made of rough-hewn wooden blocks. I talked about my travels, how my life had fallen apart, and where I had been the last decade. The women. The booze. The jobs. I joked about getting a punch card for having so many state tax returns to file. I mentioned the insatiable need; the press and drive for meaning. I told him how I felt about God and eternity. Grace and hatred.

For the first time in my life, he just sat back and listened.

I spoke rapidly, knowing that the time was limited. I knew my brother would want to say his piece and that the old man was desperate for more pain meds. His eyes were red-rimmed, strained, and getting worse by the moment. My whole tale had taken about ten minutes.

I rose to leave, but he waved me down. The nurse stood up and came in through the door. He waved her off as well. This time she listened.

The remaining muscles in his neck, if you could call them that, pulsed and rippled. He was trying to speak and couldn't. His eyes finally met mine. Eternity passed as we stared at one another. It was over in a blink. And then he was writing. When he turned the whiteboard back around it read, simply:

"I'm sorry."

His eyes were wells of pain, boundless. Tears flowed openly down his face. He reached up and furiously wiped them away. I wanted nothing more in the entire world than to see those eyes find peace. But there was nothing I could do...

You can hate someone so virulently that your entire life is built off of it. I know this very well. I have gone through those seasons. But our greatest enemies are simply the ones that have the capacity to hurt us the most. And they wouldn't be able to hurt us if there wasn't anything that they could take from us.

My parents had stolen my childhood from me, making me an orphan in my own 'home(s).' This man had abandoned, neglected, and openly abused me more times than I could count. But in that moment, none of it mattered. I was proud of him for making an effort, for trying so hard when the pain was so intense. Somehow, he was easy to forgive.

I didn't have to practice anymore.

"I know," I said. "I am, too."

I rose and broke eye contact. For the last time, I reached out and touched his shoulder. There was still warmth there.

I walked into the hallway in a daze. My eyes were blurry and dull. A throbbing headache had made its way into the front of my sinuses.

Must be the bright lights.

I waved my brother into the room. We didn't need to speak. We had taken turns for our entire lives. He knew the drill.

My memories after that aren't reliable. At some point, we were checking into the hotel. Sometime the next day, we went back to the hospital. This time our father was thoroughly incapacitated. We spent time with his partner and watched his chest feebly rise and fall. And then it was time to go.

I don't remember the drive home, or the flight later that evening. I don't remember having to get a hotel because my girlfriend had forgotten to pick me up. And I certainly don't remember missing my shift the next day.

I stuffed it down. As deep as it would go. No one believed that I had gone down to see my dying father. Instead, they had crafted a story wherein I was fixing to quit; to get out from under my contract. I was suddenly aware of how tenuous my position there had become. It was only days 'til my vacation. I drank Kahlua with my coffee and Tito's with my water. I cussed at customers and padded my tips. Nothing mattered. Under it all, a phrase reverberated, like the dull tone of a large bell extoling the time.

Not so bad, Dad.

Not so bad, Dad.

Not so bad...

19

Nowhere, Montana

It started with a kiss.

Actually, it started with some good old-fashioned stalking on her part, but I'll never have a better opportunity to start a story with that sentence.

After weeks of avoiding the inevitable, I was given a golden opportunity. We were alone on an empty patio underneath a full set of stars and a brazen, half-lidded moon. The crashing of waves drowned out all other sounds. I took full advantage. She kissed me back with intensity. I felt like I was drowning and being uplifted into the sky at the same time. Things happened quickly after that.

Her name was Delilah. She was beautiful, scatter-brained, and lived the life of my dreams. I had her on a pillar so high that even a Roman Emperor would be wondering about my sanity. She would eventually become my wife.

We didn't know that then. We played the usual games: running away from each other, lying, and trying to hide our insecurities. It didn't matter. The attraction was stronger than our coping strategies. Our games always resulted in the same outcome. We were together, for better or worse.

The next two months were a whirlwind that is hard to fully sum up with human language. Writers far better than I have tried for thousands of years to adequately explain the span of human emotions while we're in love. Shakespeare flew close to the sun, but even that is still measured in astronomical units. Take a moment and think of the last time you were impossibly in love... Yeah, it was like that.

The moment that I knew I was catastrophically fucked came at a bar. It was our first real date. I'd arrived early and was anxiously pounding vodka tonics and talking with some acquaintances when she walked in. The music stopped. At least, it did for me. I set down my drink and forgot what I had been saying mid-sentence. She had high heels on and a skin-tight dress, perfectly molded to her frame. Everything I had ever been through in life suddenly seemed fair, just, and appropriate.

Worth it.

I stood, walked to her, and froze. Her smile lit up the coldest, loneliest parts of my existence. I could have grown a lemon tree down there. My head swam, thick with the ringing of fate. I tried to think of something clever or suave to say. Mumbled garbage was all that came out. My neck was hot around the collar as I slipped a hand around her waist and led her outside. I found that I couldn't breathe. For a moment, all that I could see was the perfectly sculpted cleavage and the 'come-get-me' grin she was flashing... It was all a man could do to stay sane.

We walked down the block, took a right, then another right, then another... The entire town was the size of a football field, and I had been to the restaurant before, but now I couldn't remember where it was. Luckily, the manager, who was one of my regulars, was standing outside. She waved us in.

There was a table set up for us. I tried to keep my eyes on her face. It was a losing battle that I surrendered to with grace. There was a general feeling of compulsion, like two black holes merging. We both had tractor beams, locked on to one another, full power. There was no escape from this. And somehow that was a comforting feeling.

I knew all of the cooks, the bartender, the host... We ordered the menu, including sake, and were bombarded with extras and friendly banter. I got to look like the biggest big shot in town. I barely noticed. She was simply sitting there, smiling, with her hands between her shimmering dress. I picked up a piece of sushi and held it towards her. She grinned, bit it off of the chopsticks, and flashed a rice-y grin. It was the most beautiful thing I had ever seen in my life.

Not so bad...

***

The deck of my apartment looked right over the lake and the bar below. I usually had a fully stocked liquor cabinet and a fridge full of beer. Today was no exception.

I cracked my first can of the evening and palmed the letter. There was something symbolic about the paper. I had left countless jobs before. I had quit, been fired, forgotten to even show up, and had generally gone through the grinder of corporate and small-business America as thoroughly as someone can. This was different. This was like breaking up with a family member; getting ready to tell them that they were no longer going to be a part of my life. But it was necessary. They'd already hired my replacement. I wasn't wanted anymore.

My phone chimed. It was a message from Delilah, who had left for California a few days before. I'd written her a long email, telling her how I felt. The text hung on the screen like bird shit on a previously clean car window.

"Did you really expect me to stay?"

I drained the beer and walked down to the bar. Mike was behind the counter, waving and hopping around on his single leg. He was faking it that night. I knew him well enough by then to know.

Something had been bothering him the past month. We had become close. He was yet another male role model that I couldn't bring myself to actually *let in*. But that didn't faze him. He smiled at me, spun his finger a few times while pointing at the ceiling, and slid my drink of choice down the bar without me asking. I grabbed it, turned to the two owners sitting on the corner, and dropped the piece of paper.

"We all saw it coming. Let's make the last part fun, eh?" I said.

The owners stared at me and smiled in unison. A long time ago, Brian had taught me how to gauge a smile. The key is to look at the eyes and then move downward. The eyes will tell you everything. Then the smile, once you know it's fake, will tell you even more. The eyes staring at me reminded me of two snakes wondering where the softest skin on my face to sink fangs into was. Their smiles told me even more. I didn't wait for a response.

Instead, I turned to Mike and ordered two shots. Mike was as big of a drunk as I was. Everyone knew that we weren't allowed to take shots while we were working. Or at all, really. This time he didn't blink. He whipped out two rocks glasses, filled them to the brim with tequila, tossed me a lime that I snatched out of the air, and we clanked and tossed them back.

Fuck 'em.

***

The bitterness was palpable, hanging in the air like a noxious gas being constantly released from the air ducts. All of the regulars, some of whom I had become good friends with, had distanced themselves from me like I had contracted the plague.

I had already been the black sheep, the hired gun that would inevitably leave when the curtain drew. Now I was Public Enemy No. 1. How *dare* he leave *us*.

I watched as people I had routinely taken care of, either with alcohol or free therapy sessions, acted like I was the equivalent of a jukebox on the wall. One woman, who I had driven home a few times when she became too drunk, began snapping at me when she wanted something. I was counting minutes and I had cut grooves into the bottom of the bar rail. After a few days of this, I got another text from Delilah:

"I'm thinking of coming back sooner."

I remember that moment with crystal clarity because that is when everything changed. Money had always ruled everything around me. It was my safety net, my means of conveyance. People were just illusory, transitory experiences; leeches that sapped my strength and the syrup of my heart, then inevitably disappointed and betrayed. All I had was my job and the road.

There were a bunch of empty glasses on the bar. I let them wait, instead choosing to stare out the broad, double-paned windows. The lake outside was placid, reflecting the distant hills with startling clarity. The sun shone over it all, casting a long, attenuated reflection out over the water. No pontoon boats or kayaks dared disturb the pristine serenity. In that moment, money didn't matter anymore.

With the finality of a sledgehammer hitting a large piece of drywall, I chose to ignore every red flag I had seen so far. Whereas the use of money as a means of seeking meaning had faded, now there was another illusory object: love. Despair had punctured my mental fabric as soon as my father had died, and the actions of the remainder of my family since then had driven hard iron spikes into the remaining grey folds. My last girlfriend had demonstrated to me that I was unlovable and my family had shown me that I was unwanted. The slow decline of my status in this bar, the first place I had truly felt at home in a decade, had reinforced that I was never, ever going to find a home. I had to find a silver lining.

I had to cling to the hope that I have always clung to: that there was a place for me in this world and that I would find a person who would love me for exactly who I was. The evidence in that crummy little town had been exactly the opposite, but the evidence be *damned*. Mentally, I shifted all of my chips from my pile to the center of the table.

And I put them on Delilah.

I trudged through the rest of the week in a triggered miasma of anxiety and hypervigilance. I was surrounded by enemies at all times. Even my home was within shouting distance of the oppressive stink of betrayal and abandonment. I was so upset that I actually slowed down my alcohol intake. I fell back into my old routine of packing my bag each night, only to unpack it the next day when I needed something. It was a means of creating the illusion of control. I could leave any time I wanted to.

But I had to hold on. Delilah's entire family lived a few towns over and she was planning on staying with them for a few weeks. I'd bought a one-way ticket to Europe and I knew I had to hang around if I was ever going to convince her to go with me. I was already planning my life around her. I had to wait.

She showed up a few days later and we were almost inseparable for the next two weeks. It was as if there had been a hole in my chest my entire life that I hadn't known was there, and every time she was within fifty feet of me it was filled to overflow. We were wild and feral, jumping into rivers, sprinting through abandoned fields, romping through parties, and tearing through the broad plains of Montana like we owned them. We would wake up with our feet hanging out the back of a Subaru, the warm summer sun tickling our toes as the mountains waved to us and birds danced across the open sky.

I was free.

***

One night, I found myself at a party on the lakeside. I had learned quickly that as long as I stayed away from my workplace, these folks were still warm and friendly. I was riding high that night, bouncing from conversation to conversation, and jumping in the lake with wild abandon.

Shortly after the sun had set, Delilah walked across the grass. When I caught sight of her, she was awkwardly standing on her tip toes, staring at me, a slight smirk hanging off her face like the tank top hanging on to her shoulders. The glow of the lamp lights from the nearby docks framed her face perfectly. I walked over and kissed her, oblivious to the people around. She pulled back and made a slight grimace, then looked down at the beer in my hand.

"Peh! Coors Light," she said. "That's the only bad one."

I smiled and poured it out on the ground, crushing the can simultaneously. With one smooth, well-practiced motion, I threw the can into a nearby trash bucket without breaking eye contact. It wouldn't have mattered if we were in the middle of a warzone, the Thanksgiving Parade, or on the moon. There was only her and I. We were the king and queen of this small slice of Earth, the future, the golden geese, the chosen ones. There was nothing else in my universe but her stout little shoulders and the weight of her stare. I would have burned that entire town to ashes if she had asked me to.

Luckily, she didn't. A few minutes later, we were hightailing it back to my house, her stepfather's car mere feet away from the plate-less jalopy I'd been driving. We pulled into my parking lot next to each other. I pulled the six pack I had left in the front seat, grabbed her hand and we head toward my house across the gravel parking lot.

There was a trailer there where the cook from the bar lived. His name was Derwin and he was the best friend of the bar owner's son. He had gotten out of prison a few months ago and had worked with us ever since. I had never asked exactly why he was in prison in the first place, but I knew it was for something violent and that he had been in there for a very long time. We were friends, of a sort. He used my shower sometimes. We had shared a lot of jokes and cigarettes. Nevertheless, he had withdrawn over the past few weeks, along with all of the rest. I knew there was some tension between us. The bar owner's son and Delilah had a complicated relationship. There were lies being told, but I was oblivious to all of them.

As I crossed the gravel parking lot, Derwin approached rapidly, smiling in a way that told me that he was intensely drunk. He reached forward and grabbed a beer out of my six pack. It wasn't that I wouldn't have given him one if he had asked. It was the way that he simply assumed that what I had was his to take. It was reminiscent of the entire town, a microcosm of how every person in the area had been treating me for months.

I stood up tall and told him to give it back. He got right in my face, a quarter inch separating us. His eyes were bright blue and frenzied, the slight sheen of insanity glazing the retinas. There had always been a deep sadness in his face. It was the same look someone gets when they have spent most of their life incarcerated. He usually reminded me of a caged animal growling at the edge of the open door, protecting the bars surrounding it.

I felt him head-butt me, but that was it. The next minutes were erased from my memory. And for good reason. For the first few days after this, I had no idea what had really happened. I thought that I had been in a fight and that I had lost. What had actually occurred was much worse.

Derwin hadn't head-butt me at all. Instead, he'd taken the beer bottle he'd been holding and brought it down on the front of my head. Then he had repeated the procedure three more times. Someone who I hadn't seen previously, the bouncer maybe, had pulled him off.

I came to still standing. I have taken some nasty hits and somehow always had the ability to stay on my feet. I tasted blood. Lots of it. I was so enraged that I tried to rip off my shirt, but it was too wet... When I looked down at my chest, all I could see was a bright red color... kind of pretty, actually... all the way down to my feet.

Ah shit. That's blood.

It was my blood, to be precise. Life was a dull thrum, the basest of consciousness, 1s and 0s flashing across the exposed command prompt. I couldn't... feel. Anything. I could hear the squelching of blood between my feet and my sandals though. Delilah was nowhere to be seen.

I rushed the guy. He had his back to me and he was wobbling back and forth like his knees were going to give way. I tackled him to the ground, pinned him, and then started throwing fists down toward his face. The problem was that they were going at least eight inches to the right every time. Someone, the bouncer maybe, gently put their hands between my armpits and lifted...

I stumbled backward. My vision spun around a central axis, like I was in the middle of a tornado and could only look out through the top... and instead of sky, all I could see was blackness. I stumbled away from the parking lot, feet trudging through the bloody gravel beneath me. I heard Derwin get in a car and spit gravel everywhere as he tore off and away.

The next thing I remember is being in my bathroom, staring at three versions of my face, all of which were straight out of a horror movie. Blood was everywhere; I was blood. I could see giant, gaping cuts on my scalp that, even through the swampy, murky haze, I knew I would have to stitch up. A bottle of Tito's appeared in my hand. Then I stepped in the shower, fell to my knees, and held the open bottle above my head.

This is going to hurt.

I managed not to scream. The vodka coated my head in a searing magma that was so painful I barely noticed when it reached my eyes. Shock and adrenaline were my only friends. I turned the water on and took a pull from the bottle. More magma. This time, it was everywhere.

It took a while to wash off my skin. Gravel had gotten everywhere, attached to my legs and arms by the sticky, viscous blood soup that I had cooked in my brain. I knew I was in trouble. I managed to clean up enough to not resemble a bloody zombie, toweled off as best I could, and then reluctantly trudged to the mirror. One of the cuts needed immediate attention. I had thread handy, as well as a needle and a lighter.

Why I didn't immediately go to the doctor, or call the police, is one of the bigger mysteries of my life. But the thing about concussions is that your mind stops making sense and reverts back to its most basic notions of how to keep you safe. I have never liked or trusted doctors, especially when I was a kid, and there was no one there to tell me different. The thought simply never occurred. I got the needle out and ran the lighter over it. Everything was going to be fine. It had to be.

It was hard to hold the cut together and puncture my own skin with the needle, but somehow I managed. The fact that I was able to establish, thread, pull, and thereby effectively suture the main cut on my head as quickly and efficiently as I did was... not natural. I could see my eyes, dull and glazed, and the reckless tilt of my neck. Something else had guided my fingers. I had to fight off a black tide as I tied off the last knot. Then I went to work dabbing antibiotic cream and gauze into the other wounds. Just as I was finishing, the sliding door opened.

Initially, I assumed it was Delilah, but I was wrong. It was the bar owner's son. What on Earth that man was thinking when he walked into my house without asking... I couldn't handle it. I wanted to kill him and his slack-jawed friend. I hated him then. I loathed the way that everything had panned out, and the way that I had been treated. I despised their inability to see past their own noses. And now, in my darkest hour, he chose to walk right into my last remaining safe haven. Enough was enough.

I let him know all of this at top volume. I screamed at him to get out and, when he declined, I punched him square in the face. My brain was child-like in that moment, completely incapable of making rational decisions. Something else stayed my hand. It was a grace that neither of us possessed. The owner's son left without a word. I spat on the door behind him, then opened it thirty seconds later, stood on the blood-stained porch, and lit a cigarette.

Eventually, Delilah returned. A thin tendril of blood was making its way down my forehead to meet the smoke wafting from my fingers as I watched her climb the stairs from the street below, stroll across the gravel, and walk past me into my apartment. I marveled at how little she cared but couldn't understand it. I desperately needed someone in that moment. What I got was... that. She looked at me almost with contempt; as if I had disgraced her by getting pummeled. Where she had been I will never know. For the remainder of our relationship, she continued to assert that she had been there the entire time.

The rest of the night was a nightmare. I couldn't sleep, obviously, and I couldn't control my emotions. I would flash with white-hot anger, then sink into the deepest, lowest pit of despair. My hands reflexively grabbed cans and glasses, more booze to drown away the horror that was present on my scalp. My hands shook violently. Delilah sat near me, half on and half off the ottoman, with her hands between her legs. She still had that look, as if I was a dog that had shit on the rug, but she was trying to hide it behind a mask of irritated concern. Sometime around sunrise, I finally laid down and went to sleep.

When I woke up, she was gone. I thought long and hard about calling the police. Something stayed my hand. I knew that Derwin was on his third strike. A crime like this would put him away for life. I had no one to call. No one to get advice from. I had to decide on my own. And my addled, concussed brain decided to be merciful. I still loved these people, despite their faults. The fact that they didn't love me back was irrelevant.

I sat on the couch and stared at the wall for hours. At some point, I received a text message from the boss. I was fired. The entire thing was so incomprehensibly insane... my head pounded as I tried to rationalize it. I grabbed the cushions as if they were going to lend some kind of support and held on, swaying back and forth, fits of nausea threatening to take over my entire body. Days passed as a confusing array of voices echoed in my mind:

C'mon. Have a beer with your old man.

This hurts, Mack.

What the hell was that?

You hear me, you little shit?

But a judge won't.

I'm sorry, Muffin.

Don't you DARE say this was your fault!

Not so bad, Dad.

Not so bad...

20

DUNEDIN

Both of my hands were over her eyes for the entire ride. I'd left the hostel in the trusted hands of an employee that I'd caught—multiple times—swapping beds for sexual favors. Thanks to New Zealand labor laws, she could remain an employee for months after she had been fired, and until this time period was up, I couldn't hire anyone else. Oh well. It was Delilah's birthday. If the place burned down, maybe I'd finally get some sleep. She squirmed underneath my hands as the cab came to an abrupt stop.

"Can I look now??" she asked, half-smiling. I sidled close. Her eyelids fluttered as my hands moved aside. When she saw the ice rink, she gasped, screamed a little, then wriggled out the door. She was still hopping up and down as I handed cash over the seat.

Inside were two rinks, aligned perpendicular to one another. Both were empty. I would have been fairly put out if they weren't, considering that I'd paid good money to rent the whole place. Two sets of skates had been laid out for us. The radio was on, blasting all of the pop hits we had flown so far to escape. Blue and purple strobe lights passed across the ice, rhythmically cutting across the dim expanse of the arena. Next to the skates was a note, written in expansive cursive:

All yours till 7 :)

She tried to jump in my arms, kiss me, and put on ice skates at the same time. Somehow, she managed all three. Within thirty seconds, she was already hobbling forward.

With one powerful lunge, off she went. One skate was pushing, the other gliding... the epitome of graceful. The ice was hers, and she used every square inch of it.

My own skates slid, slowly and clumsily, across the slippery plane. My ankles buckled and flexed as my feet skittered here and there. I was too transfixed to care.

She had grown up in Montana with a lake next to her house. Ice skating was her favorite thing to do. Her eyes would roll back in her head when she told me stories about her early morning glides.

I'd been looking for potential marketing opportunities for the hostel when I'd spotted the rink. The only problem was that it was closed for the season. I'd called three times a day anyway. To my surprise, one day someone had picked up.

She darted and flashed, loops within loops, then came toward me. Her grin was pure, unsullied. She sprayed me with ice and flashed a come-get-me grin. I gave it my best shot.

An Ed Sheeran song wafted across the stale, arid hall. I could hear her singing along as she passed the far wall. I was witnessing something, long imprisoned, be set free.

She was a wild mare, happily bucking on the open plane. It didn't matter that we fought constantly, or that the nightmares kept me up most nights. My temper and her violent mood swings took a back seat to the unbridled joy unfolding over well-groomed ice and a pastel light show.

No one will ever convince me that ice-skating is fun, but sometimes you just have to strap on your boots and finish the mission. I set out towards the middle and fell only once. I needed a better spot to take pictures from.

The skates beneath her were a blur, spinning here, cutting there. Her arms, usually so clumsy, whirled in carefully weighted spirals, fingers piercing the air. Her balance was perfect. The ice glinted and glistened in time to the plastic pop. She was grace personified.

Drool fell from the corner of my mouth. I was a wallflower at the homecoming dance, hoping the most beautiful girl in school would come and kiss me on the cheek...

Well, hot damn.

She did.

There were other things to do that night. Minigolf. Dinner. A movie. All of her favorite things. But for now, there was nothing but the sharp cold of the ice beneath, the scraping of the skates, and two chemical-riddled kids desperately trying to make it work in a foreign land.

She whipped through the arena as if she was being paid by the universe to simply traverse the plane. I stared like I was being paid to witness the transitive nature of joy. Maybe we were.

She must have gotten tired of seeing me stand there, because with two purposeful thrusts, she was at my side. This time, the ice sprayed behind me. She grabbed my hand and gently led me to the wall. I tried my best to keep the skates straight and my legs from shaking.

I looked at her then. There were concerns there, to be sure. Unresolved issues. Anger. A remarkable problem with taking accountability. But to me, the good outweighed the bad. And that was enough. I'd made up my mind what I was going to do.

"What does that face mean?" she asked, softly. She tightened her grip and veered closer. A light flicker of uncertainty passed across her face. It faded when I smiled.

"Happy Birthday, Bunny. Let's go around a few more times."

21

BLUEBERRIES

Cold. There was nothing else in our world aside from frigid, biting cold. The sun shone down in thick waves of photon-laden goodness, but none of that reached through to the row we were working on. Our arms were drenched to the shoulders. I shook violently and cursed my luck for the millionth time. We stood in thick, overgrown banks of blueberry bushes, most of them much taller than we were, picking berries as fast as we could go. That was the job that week. We were simply trying to make enough money to get to the next town. One blueberry at a time.

Running the hostel had been my dream job. I'd been in constant flow; a walking confluence of skill, talent, and passion. For the first time in my life, I truly enjoyed working. Delilah had hated everything about it. That made things pretty simple. There was also another factor that had to be considered: I had known that the owner was a bit crazy. Security cameras were everywhere—including one hidden one in the alarm clock in my room.

I'd worked myself into the ground. From dawn 'til late into the night, I was on call and on the ball. The owner had promised, countless times, expanded abilities to run the business and manage my staff. It had never materialized, which meant that the entire operation rested on my shoulders. And then, of course, the cameras.

The relationship quickly devolved. We'd left in a hurry.

Delilah was no happier on the road. As our money ran out, we began to fight ferociously. Her behavior quickly became intolerable. Tension dominated every moment. Small things turned into long term problems. I walked a high wire, forever looking for new coping strategies and outlets for my stress. But I had made up my mind. She was the one. If she acted like a child, well, that was what I deserved. Right?

In reality, it was a classic case of the sunk-cost fallacy. I saw her as a high-risk, high-reward investment, believing that I could recoup my losses if I held on long enough. The gambler mentality undercut any sense of calm rationale, despite the insistent whispers of my unconscious mind. This voice only ever said one thing:

Run.

The strain had overwhelmed everything else. I'd taken the first job I could find. That had been a week ago. I looked down at my fingers and saw narrow rivulets of blood slipping down my right wrist. My hands were a shade of pale that looked inhuman.

Delilah moved through the bush across from me. A wracking, phlegm-filled cough shook her frame. She looked at me. The contempt I had seen on her face months before had returned.

There was only one way out. I picked furiously, ignoring the pain in my hands, filling tray after tray. We just needed enough for a bus ride... If I could get us out of there... If I could find a decent-paying job... Then maybe, just *maybe*, she would love me again...

My mind spiraled. Rage bubbled up and was bluntly stuffed back down. Self-pity welled up next and met the same fate. It just wasn't fair. I had gone ten miles in her direction. She hadn't budged an inch. Times were hard.

I had told her this would happen. Why didn't she understand that some things you have to work for?

Why wasn't I *worth it*?

My hands trembled, desperately aching. Picking each berry took a Herculean effort. The sky was now obscured by thick, blackening clouds. I looked up to where the sun had been. Despair sank in. I had been counting the seconds, begging for relief. I considered throwing it all in. We could just use my credit card. Buy plane tickets back to The States. Get her back to her family and...

And with a gentle, undulating tremor, the singing started.

It was a firm, rolling tide of soft harmonies and piercing melodies that crossed through the rows. I checked my wristwatch. 10 a.m., on the nose. The bells from a nearby church tolled, echoing out over the lush, sweeping hills that surrounded the farm. Row after row of workers sang the hymns in unison. The ice-cold chill was replaced with reverence and joy that reverberated through the rows. Suddenly, it dawned on me: it was Sunday.

I stopped and looked across the row. Delilah had paused, one translucent hand held above a juicy branch. She was standing up straight, her cheeks flushed with a bright pink, a smile worming its way across her lips. When she saw me looking, she stared me full on in the face. Behind the exhaustion, there was a faint glimmer. It was the only opening I was likely to get.

Without thinking, I crossed straight through the bushes between us. Thick branches caught on my coats and whipped back into my face. Everything stung as I grabbed her by the waist. She started to resist, slapped at the outside of my arms, then sighed. I started to lead her in a slow dance, round and round in circles. Blueberries, sodden and heavy, fell around us in clumps.

Then we were laughing, spinning round and round, purring in each other's ears. The hymns rolled over us. Our animosities and grudges were just wrinkles, smoothed by the warm blanket of other people's faith. We were back on that dock, two star-crossed lovers kissing for the first time. I raised her chin and planted one on her, potent and insistent. I could feel the warmth that I had sorely missed. She was a tall glass of water and I was bone-dry and lost in the desert. A flicker of hope rose through my spine. If we could get through *this*... well, we could get through anything.

The hymns lasted all day. We worked like mad, furiously stacking crates, both of us knowing instinctively that this was our last day there. The constant bickering was replaced by warm advances and gentle touches as we passed. Her hand rested on my thigh as we ate our peanut butter sandwiches and stared at the grey skies above. I knew that it would take more than hymns to save us. But for now, they were enough.

The next day, our first paychecks were deposited into our accounts. I had awoken with the sun, made coffee, and sat hunched over the screen, scouring job boards. When she began to stir, I thrust the screen in her face, pointing to the bottom line. The amount we had earned was surprising. We had picked a lot of blueberries. It was over. She reached across the blankets and drained what was left of my coffee.

"Where to next?" I asked.

"Anywhere but here," she replied.

She rose, stark naked, and headed for the shower. I reached for her but she didn't see my hand. Something stirred in my memory. There was something... *familiar* to all of this. I dismissed it. We were exhausted and needed a fresh start. That was all. I listened to the sounds of the water as I booked the train tickets, then began packing my bag.

22

Yellowstone

No one likes to admit how close they have come. We prefer to focus on the meaningful, poignant, and beautiful moments of our lives. It makes for great movies and cinematic storytelling. We instinctively watch the survivors, ignoring the casualties, as a way of avoiding our own mortality. Our focus is always on life and how it will go on. It is challenging to talk about those moments when we didn't want it to. Society sees them as the ultimate weakness. Taboo. As if they aren't normal, or that they make us less human.

I have come very, very close. More than once. Sometimes something greater than me stopped my hand. Other times, it was my own self-will. I hold no shame for this. Rather, I am proud. It shows that I had shrugged away my coat of numbness and faced the world head-on. This was one of those times.

It was finally over. We'd returned to the States. Shortly after that, I had taken her down to see her father. It only took two weeks for everything to implode. I had left burnt rubber on abandoned highways from Tahoe to Bozeman, stopping at every roadside casino and ramshackle saloon along the way. Despite a trip to the mechanic, my wallet had stayed stuffed. My nights were spent falling asleep on the tailgate, a bottle of Jack Daniels between my legs, my feet grazing the warm desert ground beneath.

It happened so quickly that I'd had no idea what to do with myself. I was in a tailspin. Montana was the only place where I'd ever had any luck, so I drove north. After a week of aimless wandering, I got a buzz-cut and chopped off my beard, leaving only a bushy mustache. I bought a cowboy hat and two old pairs of jeans. Soon enough, every word I spoke was a lie. I'd created a false identity. The real version of myself was just too painful to go back to.

I met up with an old friend in West Yellowstone for a few drinks, then cut out on one of the many four-wheel roads out of town. My truck creaked and groaned as I floored the accelerator, taking the hairpin turns at reckless speeds. I was doing my best to get lost, taking random turns without keeping track. I hoped that there was a cliff somewhere, one that I wouldn't see before I was flying off of it. I was a cowboy, damn it, and I fully intended to die like one.

I soon found a place where there was absolutely no chance of being disturbed. The road was elevated and isolated, with a 360-degree view of the surrounding area. I had filled my cooler with bread, meat, and beer. The world was silent save for the occasional grasshopper. I chased my whiskey with beer, bare feet dangling off the back of the truck. The expanse before me clutched at my soul, pulling outwards, ever outwards...

When it became too cold, I pulled on my sleeping bag, and with the edge pulled up to my chin, I stared at the stars above. I wondered if she was looking up at that moment, seeing the same constellations... I wondered what she was thinking... I could see her face, feel her soft, slow breathing beside me. Reflexively, I reached out. My hand dragged across the rusted, cracking metal, spreading crushed cans, until it reached the side of the frame...

I awoke to the sun peeping over the tire well. A brisk wind sent sprays of dirt up into the truck bed.

Sometime in the early afternoon, I sat in the cab, boots on the dash, dust pouring in from the windows. My knife was firmly planted against my neck. I was going to finish my beer, then finish myself. Shimmering waves of heat wafted from the faded red paint of the hood, swimming fractals that obscured the barren dust bowl around me. My cigarette slipped from my hand onto the floor below. It might have still been lit. I didn't care.

I could feel blood trickling down my neck. My knife was sharp and broad. It was a K-Bar, stolen from my father's house long ago. I looked up at the faded beer stains on the headliner. Remnants of good times. Everywhere I looked, I could see her touch on my life. The wind itself whispered her name. I couldn't turn it off, despite how desperately I wanted to. I couldn't see past my misery, into a future where I was okay on my own...

So, this is how it ends.

I tightened my grip and steadied my hand. I tilted my head and felt the last swig hit the back of my throat. Then I crumpled the beer can...

I heard something odd. It was the sound of... was that something dragging?

Definitely. It was unmistakable. I cannot stand the sound, almost as bad as people chewing with their mouths open. A flash of annoyance flared through the despair. I had driven all this way, coming to the ass end of nowhere, just to have some little ankle-dragger ruin my last moments...

I slowly pulled the knife away and straightened. A small, dust-ridden body was trudging up the hill next to the truck. My eyes, once glazed, focused on the object in front of me. Moment by moment, the details resolved themselves. It was a kid. In the middle of nowhere. Clearly lost. Sweat stains ran deep down his elbows.

I was too stunned to do anything. It was none of my business, anyway. I watched as the kid took another fifty steps or so. What could I do? I was a drunk, suicidal man in his early 30s, sitting in the middle of nowhere, holding a knife in his hand. The kid would probably be terrified of me.

But where was he going? How did he get here? I sat and waited for a few breaths, then straightened up in the seat. Nothing moved anywhere nearby. It was hot that day. Too hot. The kid must be headed to an RV or something... It was none of my business. But something tickled. A firm hand grabbed the top of my spine. I could suddenly see. Was it... is that... duty? It was something, all right. Something besides dying.

Son of a...

I started the engine and whipped it into drive. It didn't take long to get the truck pulled around and headed after him. As I approached, the kid stumbled trying to get out of the way, almost falling into the ditch. I rolled down the window and stopped next to him.

"Hey, kid!" I yelled. He stared blankly, eyes wide. "Do you need a ride? So obviously, never get in the car with strangers. But, um, this seems like an exception."

He was already clambering in between 'car' and 'strangers.' I turned on the air conditioning and stared at him. He couldn't have been older than nine. His skin was pale and blotchy, and terror was etched around his eyes. Dust covered his bare arms and legs. I fumbled around behind the seat and pulled out a jug of water and two granola bars. He set into the jug immediately. The kid *inhaled* the water. One second later, it was half-full, as if he had discovered that osmosis was his superpower and was now using the ability on himself. He ignored the food, which was a bad sign. That meant heatstroke.

I started to roll down the road.

The AC barely worked, but it would have to do. I turned it on full blast, closed the vents closest to me, and tried to keep the kid talking. He was crowded against the far wall of the cab, half-crouched, ready to jump out the door. I didn't know what to do, so I reached beneath the seat and slowly pulled out the knife that had just been pressed against my neck. I spun it around and handed it to him, handle first. That's what I would have wanted in that situation. He took it.

"I'd be nervous in a stranger's truck too," I said. "Just make it quick, okay?"

I don't know where the words came from. I doubt they were mine. And wonder of wonders, the kid actually laughed. Then he looked at me.

I knew the expression. It was a look I had made countless times as a child. Written on his features were hopelessness, despair, and gritty determination. He had clearly been running from something, desperately trying to get over the next horizon. His eyes were muted and dull. Something had happened that had led him out there.

We started to talk. I told him that he probably had heat stroke and we had to get him somewhere to get treatment. I would definitely have to hand him over to either some kind of authority or to his parents. If we didn't, I would get arrested. He vehemently resisted that statement until he heard the end. I think he understood. No matter what happened, this wasn't going to look good. I was drunk as a skunk, driving a kid I had picked up in the middle of nowhere, with a bad-looking mustache. And the highway was at least forty-five minutes away.

The kid cried and told me about some of the things going on in his life. It dawned on me more than once that I was uniquely qualified to discuss these things with a young man; that, in fact, I might have been put in this *exact* situation for this reason. I explained to him the intricacies of what was going on in his life from the adult perspective. I told him about my experience when I was his age; about how it was most likely to play out. The kid was sitting cross-legged on the seat by now, inhaling more water and eating one of the protein bars. A pride swelled in my chest. Something momentous had happened. I'd be damned if I knew what it was though.

We got to a place where I could make a call. The kid's phone was dead, but he knew his grandmother's phone number by heart. This started a flood of phone calls from his grandmother, frantic mother, and the police. It was a torrent that I couldn't handle. I focused on the mother, and urged her to stop screaming into the phone. I told her that I was driving into the town of West Yellowstone proper and told her exactly where I would be, then called the police and told them the same. I just hoped that the mother made it before the cops, or this was going to be a very long day.

We didn't have to wait long. I stopped in the most visible part of the parking lot, then stood outside the truck smoking a cigarette. I was acutely aware of my own intoxication and the fact that I was alone with a child who had recently been reported as lost. My entire body trembled. Sometimes, that's just how it is. You have to do the right thing, consequences be damned.

I managed two drags before a minivan and a large truck pulled into the parking lot. The mother leapt from the car, the phone still glued to her ear. I put up a hand and she sprinted over. Then I waved at the kid, who seemed hesitant to get out of my truck. With another stroke of luck, he left the K-bar in the cab and jumped out of his own accord. The mother darted to him and hugged him fiercely. I couldn't help but notice that his hands remained glued to his sides. When I turned to the minivan, the grandfather was standing there. He had a hard look on his face. But it wasn't for me. He seemed to be looking at the mother...

I was nearly tackled from the side. She was now fiercely hugging me. There was no missing the smell of booze and cigarettes. I tried my best to look normal. I stood straight, accepting her gratitude with dull nods. As soon as I could, I made my way back to the truck. The engine was still running. I threw up one more wave, then began to pull out of the parking lot.

The sun was high now, slowly making its way across the sky. I watched the awkward way that the kid stood, how he sidled up to his grandparents. I held up a fist to the kid and he waved. I doubt that he got the reference. There was no joy in his face. The mother was saying something. In a flash, a memory returned. I was fifteen again, getting woken up by two assholes... I saw the kid's future, plain as day. He was in for a rough ride. I looked up at the headliner and shot up a prayer.

Please, take it easy on this kid. Please.

I nudged the gas pedal and drove directly over the sidewalk. Oops. Somehow, I managed to put the truck between the lines and stop in time for the next red light. By now, I was shaking so badly that I could barely hold the wheel in place. As I turned the corner, two police cars were turning into the parking lot. I watched the rearview mirror the entire way out of town.

By the time I found a place to pull over, I felt like I hadn't slept in days. The weariness overtook whatever I had been clinging to. I came to in the middle of a field, my legs hanging out of the side door. The heat had continued to rise unabated, but now there was a hefty breeze blowing. It cooled the sweat pouring from my naked upper body. I sat up and reached into the passenger footwell. My hand gripped the water jug. There was still some left in the bottom. As I greedily chugged it, something caught my eye. Someone had written something in the dust on the dash.

Thank you.

I stared at that until a buzzing sound interrupted the silence. My phone was ringing. It was Delilah.

23

SOMEWHERE

The truck sat in an empty parking lot, just off the highway. A tractor lazily meandered across a field ahead of us. We were always 'somewhere.' Nothing was stable. We lived day-to-day, always rushing off on a whim. But the past months had taken their toll. I was a powder keg. The tension built by the moment, only temporarily assuaged by the fervent onrush of caffeine and nicotine. I was bound to—

I was screaming. The alcohol had worn off, finally, around 9 a.m. There was a trailhead nearby and I could see people taking their dogs up the narrow, winding path. She'd been needling again, testing my defenses to see where I was weakest. Everything I said and did was wrong—everything needed correcting—everything was an apology—I couldn't breathe. The constant anxiety was chewing its way through my innards. I'd apologized, then backtracked, then apologized again. Guilt and shame clambered over one another, each with their hands wrapped around my Adam's apple—

Boom!

"Shut up, shut UP, SHUT UP!"

Over and over... and over. I knew that it was unacceptable; that I was weak and needed to control my emotions. But it felt so good. I could feel the rage, buried underneath miles of sedimentary rock, let loose into the atmosphere. I thought that I was taking my power back; that my life could suddenly be wrested back into my control. Where I had been so meek and docile, now I was a lion. I was going to say what I wanted to say. I was going to be heard.

"SHUT UP!"

She didn't see it that way. She was always ready. As the words poured from my lips, I became aware of her phone, nearly pressed into my face. It was recording. Spit flew from my mouth. But I couldn't stop. This was my revenge. My words were evil, abusive, and ear-shattering. I was out of control. She sat there, a smug smile on her face. Then she turned the phone towards herself and shrugged. Heavy, ragged breaths replaced the torrent of abuse spurting from my mouth. I was caught by the balls and I knew it.

The hurricane was over as soon as it began. I was so well-trained at this point that I knew, in the middle of my last sentence, what the punishment would be. I would get the silent treatment for at least two days, and I would then have to do something monumental to get back in her good graces. The cycle had begun anew.

I got out of the car and started walking. I knew by then to take the keys, lest she leave me there. I lit a cigarette in shaky hands. I wished I had a flask... Anything to take me out of this place; this inescapable nightmare. I had no idea what life was. I knew that love was everything. And this *was* love. It was all a process you had to go through to achieve a healthy relationship; the lumps and lessons you had to take. It was all my fault. I had to learn to not feel my emotions and to remain calm at all times. No matter what.

After fifteen minutes, I got back in the car. She was still in the passenger seat, tapping furiously on the screen in front of her. She smiled at something and turned it off.

"I'm sorry. Screaming like that is never okay," I said, looking down. My hands wrung themselves. She said nothing. Didn't even look up from the screen, dead in her hands. It was probably still recording.

"I think I need help," I whispered. She stayed silent. A few moments passed before she reached to the stereo, found a country music station, and turned up the volume.

I put the car in drive and, after a quick coffee stop, hit the highway. I drove for the rest of the day. Miles passed. We didn't speak a word. I found out that she had picked a hotel online when she pointed as we were approaching an exit sign. As we checked in, Delilah leaned across the counter and flashed the woman a bubbly smile.

"There's two beds, right?"

24

HONEYMOON

Her dress was beautiful. It was a cream white with soft fabric that hugged her hips, simple yet subtly elaborate in the slight embellishments to the hem and shoulders. She could've shown up in a white t-shirt and jeans for all I cared. As long as she said "I do," I would have completed my mission. Everything else was just a bonus.

I'd picked a small church near the river. It had a peaked roof of stained wooden beams that sloped all the way down to the ground. Mercifully, the ceremony was short. Something gnawed at my solar plexus—I told myself it was just nerves.

The officiant completely bungled the ceremony, forgetting our names multiple times and misquoting the Bible. I stared at Delilah through each gaffe. In that moment, she embodied the lofty vision I had of her: radiant, self-possessed, and immaculately beautiful. In between bouts of nausea, I felt like the luckiest man in the world.

When it came time to read our vows, I stepped in front of her like a supplicant to the throne. They had taken me weeks to write and drifted between inside jokes and poetry. To date, they were my magnum opus, my soul poured out into a thick wooden chalice. The finest ambrosia that had ever come from my fingers. I watched her start to cry... The words slowed and came to a halt, the paper fell from my hands… and then she was kissing me. It was done.

Almost.

The rest of the day was a flurry. Her sisters insisted on taking pictures and they refused to include me in any of them. Luckily, we had a photographer who insisted that the groom be in some of the photos taken that day. I counted minutes, trying to keep my head high. I knew that I had made a deal with the Devil, that I had sacrificed something I didn't understand.

But I was a married man. And that was all that mattered, right?

Right?

***

All of our guests arrived at once. A cacophony of sound rattled the massive cabin. Everyone was yelling and screaming, kids hung from the railings, and bags clattered up and down the stairs as they all picked their rooms. There was a feverish intensity that buzzed through the air, dripping from the walls like hot honey down the side of a glass.

Within minutes, alcohol was flowing. Delilah and I started making margaritas, and someone brought out a karaoke machine. Our mothers roosted and preened, actively avoiding one another. Life is a mirror. And the two women adamantly didn't like what they saw in one another. Still, the peace held, somehow. When my mother checked out for the evening, she kissed us both on the cheek and slipped a box into Delilah's hand.

Others left at the same time. We walked out to wave goodbye. Massive, thickly boughed trees pelted the ground with heavy drops. We waited until each car passed through the narrow, winding driveway. As we made our way inside, her brother appeared from nowhere. He wanted to talk. Delilah kept hold of my hand and looked at me. I waved her off. It was my wedding day. What could go wrong?

It turned out that he wanted to open up about his life. It was a weird time and place for it, but I took it as a welcome step in our relationship. As we talked, he slammed back beers. We all usually tried to keep track of his pace, considering how violent and unpredictable he became when drinking. When he was finished, a sigh of relief slipped from my chest. I felt like I had dodged a bullet.

The night carried on. At some point, I grabbed my brother's shoulder, looked him in the eye, and told him that I forgave him and that I loved him. He looked at me quizzically, said nothing, and walked away. He'd come to the wedding empty-handed and, shortly after, left the same. I watched him go, my heart slowly breaking. Delilah appeared at my side, her soft neck gently folding as she placed her head on my shoulder. She found my hand and gripped it strongly. This was new. I leaned into her and let her hold me up for a moment.

By midnight, we were all thoroughly drunk, the children were long put to bed, and Delilah was snoring in the master bedroom. I had just laid down with my new bride, running my hand through her hair. I watched her sleep and smiled.

I thought of how far we had come and how far we would go. The painting company that I had started was beginning to see some success, and I had bought a condo with the money my father had left me. I would be getting the keys from the realtor the following day. I had officially turned a corner, and could finally live the life of my dreams. I chalked up my anxiety to the normal jitters that come with massive life changes.

I had just slipped under the covers when the front door slammed violently, sending puffs of dust falling from the rafters. This was followed by more slamming, this time from the kitchen. It was her brother, yelling as loud as he could.

"THERE'S NO DAMN SNACKS 'ROUND HERE."

Steps pounded from high above. I could hear Ted, Delilah's step-father, gently urging—pleading. More sounds came from the house. The other guests were stirring above. Thoughts fled as I rolled, got out of bed, and stepped into the kitchen.

I told him, in no uncertain terms, to get out. An argument about whose house it was ensued. He could barely stand straight. He wanted to 'step outside.' On this night, of all nights, he wanted to fight me. I turned around, slammed the door, and began to lie down again. Delilah didn't stir. A loud snore erupted from her chest cavity—

Suddenly, he was in our room, yanking on my foot. A murderous shade of red cast down over my eyes as I rose. I saw his death, felt his pulse ebbing...

I reached to my side and slid the K-bar from underneath my pillow...

Before I could blink, Ted had appeared and gruffly dragged my drunken brother-in-law from the room. I didn't care. I took one step forward...

...and slammed the door. A voice came through the haze. This time it was my own.

You signed up for this.

It was over. We were married. And that was all that mattered.

25

SPIRAL

I knew it was broken. But it couldn't be. Not here. Not now. I was down, my right leg caught between two rocks that had slid along with me in an awful version of a baseball slide. I had been hurrying, jumping from rock to rock, dancing along the burnt red stones as if calling down rain.

I was in rehab. Well, we called it that off-hand. It was a shamanistic treatment center for PTSD and other notably un-fun events. Instead of psych assessments and lounging by the pool, there was yoga and meditation in the morning, vegetarian meals, and daily meetings with shamans who worked on your energy fields. It was completely nonsensical hocus-pocus. It was also the most effective treatment I've ever experienced.

Part of the treatment was to immerse oneself in the stunning glory of nature. This is fairly easy to do in Sedona. The shamanic view is that the natural world is the source of the energy within us. There are locations where this energy is stronger than others. And these are the places where we go to rid our souls of the demons that had doggedly tormented us for the majority of our lives. We'd been taken to one such location and let loose.

It's just a sprain.

I tried to pivot the leg to a normal position. That hurt. I knew pain. I had flown over the handlebars, been beaten, thrashed to pieces, kicked in the dirt, and pushed down flights of stairs. This was different. My leg just didn't *work*. It couldn't be. I was here to heal. It couldn't be broken.

Denial is a bitch.

I tried to stand. I had never seriously injured either of my legs before. I had always assumed my lower half was indestructible. No sprained ankles, no *plantar fasciitis*, nothing aside from a few broken toes. So, when I instinctively tried to put weight on both legs at once to rise up, my right immediately screamed in protest, and back down to the charitable rock I went.

I looked over my left shoulder and saw two tourists standing on the rise I had just left. They were looking right at me and pointing. I waved and tried to yell for help.

I had never done this before. I was an immutable force of nature, bound only by my own self-imposed limitations. I needed nothing and nobody. Everything was someone else's fault and I was separate from karma, society, and the world at large. I was above it all.

My first attempt was hoarse, barely audible. The shame crept up and bloomed in my voice box, infusing my cry with furtiveness and grief. I tried again, louder this time. And again, even louder. The tourists kept staring. I could see their fear. Then they fled from the rise. In the other direction.

Shit.

The enormity of the situation suddenly hit me with the force of a meteor hitting a mountaintop. This canyon was known as a place with strong feminine energy. It had been a 'birthing canyon,' where ancient women had come to bring forth countless new generations. I was caught. I could no longer deny the other side of my being. I would either surrender or I would die in agony, pinned to a rock no one would find for days.

"HELP!"

Over and over. Again and again.

"HELP!"

I cried. In shame. In anguish. In terror. I cried for what I had become; what I had *to* become. I knew I had to let go of... everything. My marriage was over. My identity was dead. My youth was gone. Who was I now? What would I do with my life? What is my purpose? How can I possibly let it all just... go?

"...help..."

With a sickening veer, everything shifted. A tsunami five hundred feet high of ego and instinct powered across the oceans of consciousness. I had survived worse than this. I had fought life to a ragged and bloody standstill on dozens of occasions. They had tried to murder me, poison me, beguile and rob me. And I had always walked out on my own two feet. I needed nothing. Nobody. There was only one way out. I fumbled my hand through the sagebrush and scrabble until I found a stick big enough, then jammed it between my teeth.

This is going to hurt.

I firmly planted and stood. Immeasurable agony lanced up my leg. I was a bundle of nerves tossed onto the grill to sear and burn. Electricity and fire coursed through the wiring. There was nothing untouched; every bone shattered into shards. I bit clean through the stick and into my tongue. No matter. There was only one way out. It was a trail of fire, no different than anywhere else I had been thus far. One step.

Two.

Every other footfall was a self-contained supernova, caught inside of a snowflake, surrounded by a cadre of ephemeral ghosts chanting in a language nobody understands. Eternity in a moment. Birth and death conjoined. I was nothing and everything. And this reality was tattooed on the membrane of every furious cell in my body. I could feel my eyes bulging, as if trying to eject from this hellacious existence. Something deeper, behind the curtain and underneath the mask, was calmly chuckling.

This is going to hurt.

I can't remember how far I made it before they came. Maybe fifty feet, maybe a thousand. Regardless, they came. My buddies, racing up the trail, panic in their eyes. I could barely speak.

"What's wrong?" one asked. A flood of questions followed. These were men I had met days earlier, yet I seemed to have known my entire life. These damn shamans might be onto something.

"Sprained. My. Ankle," I croaked. Their eyes slid down to my leg and back up. I could feel my strength bleeding into the red dust beneath... I fell.

Hands appeared around me. Pulling. Hefting. Lifting. I was adrift on the muscles of others. I couldn't stop trying to hop along, resolute that I was somehow still in control. The path was narrow, winding, and boulders jumped out from every corner and cranny. The grasping arms didn't give me an inch, clutching my weight as if they were clinging to the side of a mountaintop.

The trail finally widened as we reached the bottom of the slope. The adrenaline had fully kicked in. I could feel my ankle swelling and pulsing, already stretching the seams of my boots. People were everywhere. Children grasped and gawked. I was delirious with pain and pretense. I smiled and waved as they passed.

"It's okay, little one. Don't be afraid." I said to them.

I could feel the rabid insanity in my eyes and the grass in my hair. I clutched the hovering arms as they passed. I was hopping along, desperately trying to force the world to acknowledge the grim reality that I was indestructible; that I was unassailable; that I was righteous on my path; that I would never succumb to the frailty of man. It hurt worse with every step.

When we got back to the van, I was met with a mixture of pity, contempt, and irritation. Something about that inspired me to call my wife. I tersely explained the situation. Her replies were short, clipped, and measured, as if there was someone else listening. I could hear the contempt dripping from the speaker into my ears. I needed her then, so far away, to be human for a moment, to forget all of the issues and trauma that she kept around her like a shawl. Just once, I needed her to drop the bullshit and be a wife. To not shut down. To not run down the stairs… I heard a can cracking in the background as I hung up.

I came back to the inside of the van and focused. The hellbent desperation to launch myself at my problems returned. I could make a difference. I could reverse my life and pull a rabbit out of the fox den. I could deadlift the people I loved into transcendence. I could…

It's just a sprain.

The next day, I fashioned a cane out of a wizened old branch and hobbled from yoga, to lunch, to group… sharp needles of torture shot up my leg with every step. My ankle was five times its normal size, already a dizzying array of purples, yellows, reds, and blues…

I awoke on a thin, purple mat. A worn bronze statue of Ganesha stood poised above my left shoulder, hand raised in compassion. A middle-aged couple circled the room with various colored bowls, tapping and tolling, creating a myriad of frequencies and vibrations that coated the twenty-odd people lying haphazardly across the floor.

The head honcho was kneeling next to me, kind eyes patiently waiting for me to come back to the room. It was a safe place, held by gentle, loving hands. Within, the shrill cry of pain was constant, like a young child left to wail in the attic, the bellows seeping through the walls with each heartbeat.

He whispered in my ear for a while. I lay and listened, too exhausted to fight anymore. When I tried to shake my head, hands appeared. The woman who had previously been holding a massive ringing bowl was now standing next to my wounded ankle. She looked down once and shook her head. I looked back into the man's eyes and nodded. He was visibly relieved as he walked from the room. Something deep inside finally relaxed. Shame, powerlessness, and severely atrophied grace seeped through the searing miasma.

It might be broken.

It was. A teacher had driven me into the hospital, where a nurse was already outside tapping her foot in obvious impatience. I was rushed to the X-ray machine. The nurse clucked and *tsked*, rambling on about infection and the foibles of man. Fifteen minutes later, a man came around the corner and shook his head as he smiled.

"I'm just the tech, mind you, so I have no business telling you this, but that thing is *broken*, my man. You're lucky it didn't shatter." He rubbed his hands on his thighs twice, then he was gone.

The rest of the appointment was a blur. Images made it through the shroud. The doctor tracing a finger over the spiral crack that danced mischievously up my fibula. Ligaments... tendons... something was torn.

The man spoke quickly. Did I want pain meds? Who was my emergency contact? How was I going to get back home?

It was broken. There was no home. My business would fold. There was nothing waiting for me. Everything had to go. Including me. A cannonball had burst through the ramparts of the ramshackle sandcastle that I had erected. With one fell slide, I had been snapped, rolled, and tossed away. There was no going back.

This is going to hurt.

26

Don't Go Far

Of course, I had to go back. Things had to be done. I'd seen through the veil. I couldn't go on the way that I had. My ankle was tertiary to the spiritual journey I had to embark upon. At that point, it was simply a matter of what I could bring with me.

She had driven down to pick me up a week early. The idea had been that we could go to some groups together, meditate, do yoga, and attend some couples therapy appointments. She wanted nothing to do with that.

"I want to go back to the way things were," she said. Her back was turned and she sat on the bed opposite from me. My dog lay atop my leg, straddling it, constantly licking at my walking boot, as if that would do a damn thing. I reached over and rustled his ears anyway. At least he was trying.

The shamans took turns pulling me aside. They seemed to think that both she and my mother were going to actively try to recreate the same dynamic that had existed before I left. They were absolutely sure that I was headed straight for a train wreck. I shrugged them all off.

The last to try was my counselor. I sat in her office, assorted crystals laid out on the table before us, the smell of sage heavy in the air. Delilah had left in the middle of the appointment. As soon as the door closed behind her, the woman leaned forward in her chair, eyes dripping with intensity.

"Is this what you want?" she asked. I stuttered. My choked response was unintelligible. The realization suddenly dawned. For the first time, I wasn't sure.

I still acquiesced when Delilah asked if we could leave a few days early. I couldn't do most of the activities and she felt guilty about doing them without me. Plus, it was a long drive for one person. It made sense. We were fighting before we made it to the highway.

Things happened quickly once we returned. The house was put on the market, the business folded, my truck bartered into gold and silver. A virile impetus pushed events forward, like something was furiously holding the 'fast forward' button of an old VCR. Scant months passed and there I was, the smell of pine and motor oil permeating the air, a persistent drizzle seeping into my walking boot. I loaded my go-bag, laptop, and shotgun into the back, shut the tailgate, and turned back to the condo.

It had been my first home, with its sharply ramped ceiling cut off by the standalone fireplace and the garden I had built in the alleyway. Now it stood empty, inviting its new owner. It was a joyous day for me. The market was booming and we had made money off of the sale. There would be no more neighbors or drunken HOA presidents. I could get away from my family and start the healing process. Delilah saw it differently.

I walked through the front door to see Delilah standing in the middle of our former living room. A blue dress, my favorite, swirled around her ankles. She was lost in thought, glumly staring up at the ceiling and walls. Tears flowed across her cheeks. Her eyelids were red and puffy. Confused, I reached out to her. She pushed me away. My walking boot slid across the floor and I caught myself on the fireplace. Her eyes were glued to the short hallway to our former bedroom. She cried, standing there touching the walls, saying nothing.

"Take your time, Bunny," I said quietly. I leashed up our dog and walked out the front door. I didn't look back.

She was still crying when she got into the packed car. This time, however, there was a grim resolve. She turned to me with a smile that I would come to know well. It almost looked like the real thing.

As soon as we turned onto the road, she turned up the music. The highway was seconds away. As I floored the accelerator, an ancient sigh released itself from my chest. It had been held a very long time. Relief flooded my senses and a chill shot up through my spine. Everything was going to be alright. It had to be.

The pedestal that I had her on *had* shortened. The first glimpses of who she really was had started to seep through. My ego still held the reins of my life, however, with iron-clad talons. I told myself, over and over, that it was only a matter of time before we fixed things. It was a desperate attempt to convince myself that she loved me for more than what I possessed, that the words coming out of her mouth weren't just the last smoke from a dying fire. I had to believe that our marriage hadn't died the moment we walked out of that condo.

I couldn't deny that things had changed between us. The subterranean current that had always propped us up had been dammed and redirected, leaving ice and stone in its place. We barely touched. Her hand jerked away when I tried to cross the divide. Every hotel had two beds. The excuse was that I tossed and turned so often due to my leg, and that this kept her awake. It was a lie that she embraced wholeheartedly. I chalked it up as growing pains.

Denial is a bitch.

***

Her brother was already in the driveway as we approached. Delilah and her sister had known that he would be. They'd also known what he was going to do. Neither had bothered to tell me, though.

I was under the impression that I would be treated as a hero, as someone who had yet again treated these girls to a fantastical journey, and brought them home safely. The trip hadn't been cheap and I'd paid for everything. They'd wanted to go thousands of miles, dropping into various states to see cool places, take pictures, and eat well. Social media trembled at the amount of content they produced. Occasionally, one of them, typically her sister, would offer to take my picture. I always posed with my dog. He was happy to join me.

But my impression had been dead wrong. Her brother was storming, black clouds of rage storming above his head, unspent animosity storming out of every orifice. I assumed it was an issue between him and his mother. These folks were always fighting. That is what happens when you have an entire family of people who believe that defects should be swept under the rug like pesky little termites. The thing about termites, though, is that if you see one, there are many, many more, and it is almost guaranteed that eventually, the house will fall down around you.

Delilah popped out of the car immediately and ran inside. Her brother then tromped over and began violently pulling bags out of the trunk. I was exhausted. It had taken two consecutive ten-hour days of driving to get there. That's why it took me a few moments to realize that the anger the brother was expressing was directed at me.

He had been told about my trip to Arizona and had drawn his own conclusions. I looked to my dog, who had walked around the corner. His ears were pinned to the sides and his teeth were bared. I darted around the corner of the vehicle just as his front paws began to track toward the man, stepping in front and sealing him in against the tailgate. I could feel his tail, rigid against my ankle.

"We need to TALK, FAGGOT." The brother snarled.

As he spoke, I busied myself rearranging the bags left in the trunk. There was nothing I wanted to do more than 'talk.' I wanted to break every bone in his face. Slowly. Surgically. But I had worked hard to rid that type of thinking from my system, and I would be damned if I was going to let him... My hand just so happened to be on my shotgun, fully loaded.

It all dawned in a flash. This was a set-up, carefully planned by Delilah. I wondered if the wedding had been the same... The man before me had been prepped and used. Just like me. She had gotten to go everywhere she wanted. And now, safe inside, she left me to the dogs.

Luckily, I had one of my own. A swift, icy wind picked up, swirling dust around the back of the tailgate. I could hear the tinkling, twinkling sound of wind chimes. The childlike man before me kept rattling off insults, but they were muffled, distorted, as if he were speaking underwater.

I took a long, deep breath in... then exhaled. Then again. And again. Something stood next to me. Kind. Compassionate. Understanding. I had felt it cinched into that crack on the side of Mt. Reynolds, and on the hospital bed in Mancora. I had felt it again with the knife against my neck in Yellowstone. I could *feel* it...

A cool pressure shot down my spine. A warmth came over my eyes, and the swirling tumult turned into a personal hemisphere of breeze, encompassing like a warm embrace. It was as if there were two impossibly soft hands on either of my shoulders, sliding down my arms affectionately. Something cooed in my ears.

Don't.

I released the gun, grabbed a leash, and quickly looped it around the agitated pit bull glued to my leg. I took another deep breath and slowly exhaled. The weight of everything that had been on my shoulders slipped off in a giant plunge, like a layer of snow washing off of a metal roof in one, swift cascade. Then I started laughing.

By now, Delilah had heard the commotion she had caused and was making a big show of 'getting in the way' of her brother. I could see that she was faking. I didn't care anymore. Something had cut the cord, broken the chain.

He couldn't hurt me anymore. None of them could.

"I am not afraid of you," I said. And I wasn't. I laughed openly in his face. This only enraged him further. He kept lobbing names and insults. What else was new? I saw, firsthand, what he had thought of me the entire time; what they had all thought. I saw how much time I had wasted on this family. I saw it all, and laughed.

Their mother finally appeared, wearing the same face as Delilah. I had convinced myself that I had married the black sheep, but in reality, I had married the protégé. She made a big show of profusely apologizing. More lies. The choreography was off and the power had failed, leaving only lip-synching phonies on stage. I made sure that all of Delilah's stuff had been unloaded, then re-started the engine. Before I could get back in the car, Delilah came up to me.

"I am *with you*. He is an *asshole*. You didn't deserve that. We're a team. It is me and you. Against the world."

Lip-synching. Lies. I wouldn't be fooled any longer. When she asked if I wanted her to come with me, I told her to do what she wanted. I knew what that was. I almost asked what his name was, but stopped myself.

I made it a few hours down the road, then grabbed a hotel. And for the first time in a very long time, I walked into a bar. Pop country blasted from cheap speakers. The clientele looked as run down as the chipped, crusted stool I sat on.

"Tequila and soda. Tall. Two limes," I said as the bartender approached. I recognized her from somewhere. I had probably been there before, long ago. She looked me up and down, her sagging face losing more of its battle with gravity with each passing second. I nodded and pointed to the bottle of Hornitos on the shelf.

"And don't go far."

27

Buyer's Remorse

After a few more months on the road, we'd crash-landed in North Carolina. My leg wasn't healing, and Delilah's extracurricular activities were starting to become more obvious by the day. I could feel my engine wearing down, the teeth fracturing amidst the gears. I studied the map. Asheville would have to be good enough.

The faint whispers had turned into full-throated bellows by now. The hair on the back of my neck never went down at night, regardless of which bed I slept in. It was impossible to relax. Anxiety tore at the brackets, unscrewing the bolts of the framework. I blamed the feeling solely on the trip we had just taken. I found us a new condo and put an offer down. The bellows became high-pitched screams.

Denial is a bitch.

My leg hadn't healed correctly. Instead of fusing together, the bones had healed independently. The doctor said it was a miracle that I could still walk. The shamans said that there was a dark energy, sapping my life force. I couldn't tell who to listen to. I had distanced myself from all of my friends. My relationship with my family was nonexistent. I busied myself with moving into my new condo and throwing myself into trying to find my purpose. Everything seemed to be going well until I slipped a disc in my back.

***

My dogs shook themselves awake and stretched in unison. My laptop was knocked to the right, meaningless letters sprawled across the page. I could hear my 4Runner idling in the driveway. I squirmed out of the puddle of bodies, the heating pads sliding from my back, leg, and ankle. Through the window, I could see her face illuminated by the phone in front of her.

She smiled and put it down. Then her face changed. It always changed when she came inside.

The door slammed behind her as she entered. She was dressed nicely, in different clothes than the ones she had left in. Her hair was done up, makeup flawless. She had rarely worn makeup in Portland. There was a slight sway to her movements, but her steps were sure and swift. She didn't look at me as she crossed the living room.

"You're a piece of shit," she said, offhandedly, already disappearing around the corner. Her bags fell to the ground. "I should find a real man."

She was speaking to empty air, of course. She rarely looked me in the eye. Between the plants dotting the windowsill, the pastel reds and pinks of the setting sun cascaded across the sky. Despite the tranquility out there, the peace inside had been shattered. This was a Cold War, carried out with proxy forces in a foreign country.

"And the traffic was so bad!" she added, suddenly appearing. The dogs ran to her, tails wagging, each jumping up to her hip. She bowed slightly, her hand falling to each of their heads in turn. Something was missing... her wedding ring. She'd forgotten to put it back on.

The fog had burned away. I knew what she was doing, what she was. I tried to see her the same way that I had years before; a flighty, vacuous hummingbird, flitting from branch to branch. I clung to my vows and sense of duty like a sword in the darkness. I knew better, but it is almost impossible to drop the sword when you cannot see what is in front of you.

Denial is a bitch.

She went straight for the shower. When she returned, the dogs were back in their usual place, cuddled up against one of my legs. Neither stirred as she settled in at the far end of the massive couch. We weren't just on different ends of the room. We were on different planets. She put a Hallmark movie on and settled in, a full glass of wine in her hand.

It didn't take long before she was swiping again. I could see the reflection of it in one of the pictures still hanging on the wall to her right. She usually took down the pictures of us together. I could see other men's faces darting across the glass in the background.

"Anything we should talk about, honey?" I asked.

My back locked up then, and my hands started shaking. The leg was one thing. The bulging disc was another. Hot, molten metal pushed through my pores. This wasn't agony. This was instant death, searing through my nervous system, cruelly keeping me just at bay from the beckoning maw... She scowled at me and didn't respond. Her fingers moved closer to the screen and started to type.

The characters in the movie were still mindlessly chattering when she finished her third glass of wine. I added the last sentence to the chapter I was writing, slowly closed the laptop, and took a good, long look at her. Something had changed. She had gained weight, a lot of it, and her face was drawn and haggard. But that didn't bother me as much as... she was now more of *herself*. And that version of her, free of the masks, pomp, and circumstance, was repulsive. Where once there had been the illusion of kindness and generosity, now there was only spite and vitriol. She couldn't help herself. She had gotten what she wanted: a house with two dogs. And now I was just extra baggage in the way of her living her life.

"Delilah, we need to talk."

"About what?" she said, her face not leaving the screen.

"What are you looking at?"

The fight started immediately. Alongside the usual staple of insults, she had begun to pepper in psychological quotables. The irony was that she was describing her own behavior. It was propaganda she'd picked up on social media, an attempt to keep me off balance and unstable. But I couldn't be bothered to figure it out on my own. I was weak, physically and mentally, thinking that my lack of reaction was a form of strength. Typically, she would push until I shut down. Through my apathy, I had become a coward. I still thought it was normal.

The dogs shuffled and yawned. They always became uncomfortable when the tension rose. The room, filled with muted light from the lamp behind me, became ominous and oppressive. I had learned in couples' counseling to take breaks, get in touch with my emotions, and respond rationally to her attempts to rile me. The counselor had known what she was. He'd also known that I was a powder keg; prone to tectonic explosions of pent-up anger. He'd made sure to emphasize the fact that I needed to be assertive and take space when necessary. I did so. She followed.

"You're just projecting your insecurities on me," she said.

"You're such a piece of shit," she said.

"You're just like your *father*," she said.

I had walked into my office, locked the door, and crossed to the corner. I stood there, breathing heavily, until she pried the lock and let herself in.

There was nowhere to go. She stood in front of the door and continued the assault. I went to the only place I had left: the little chunk of my brain I had developed when I was a child. The closet in my mind.

I don't remember getting past her. She blocked my way, pushing me back once, until I forced my way through the door. The thin-paneled wood hit me in the back as I walked through it, no doubt the result of her kicking it. I rushed past the scared faces of the dogs and into the kitchen. My instincts were on full-alert. I needed my phone, something to record—

She came around the corner, wound up, and hit me as hard as she could in the shoulder. She had hit me before. It was usually an open palm, upward motion of the fist, toward my face. This was always followed by immediate denial. To her, it had never happened. And, despite the fact that it hadn't happened, it was my fault. I was so downtrodden, awash in a sea of self-pity and gluten-free beer, that I accepted everything she said to me. This time, there was no apology.

She had been aiming at my face. It was my fault that she had missed.

I stared at the pile of mail in front of me. All I could see were my hands. As long as they stayed still, I would be fine. Something cold and callous was brewing in the depths. I knew this feeling. I stared at the wall in front of me as she breathed heavily at my side.

Finally, I looked over to her. It wasn't the violence that shook me. It was the fact that I couldn't pretend anymore. I looked into her face, chaos swirling across her features, and *saw*. This wasn't The Dream. This was a prison sentence. I quickly dodged around her and made it halfway to the door before she caught my wrist.

She began wildly flailing it against her forehead. I felt the bones in my hand pop, then crack. And like bubble wrap caught between a bicycle tire, sharp, searing bursts flared through my shoulder. Another loud pop, then a bone next to my clavicle cracked back into place.

"Why don't you just hit me like you want to?!?" she screamed.

I gaped, my hand still limply flapping. In the corner, the dogs were huddled on the couch, watching the scene. I jerked my hand back, sending spasms of pain that cracked across my veins like heat lightning.

Everything hurt, yet was numb at the same time. I stood across from Hate Incarnate. I couldn't understand then that it wasn't me she hated. It was herself. More insults followed as I walked out the door onto the deck.

My hands still shook as I lit my third cigarette. She came outside. She wanted to apologize. She had been wrong to say those things. I heard her words trail off from a distance. A duality of wants and needs left me deeply confused. I wanted nothing more than to hold her, to cradle her back into peace and safety, to love her like I so desperately needed. I also wanted to leash up the dogs, pack a bag, and leave that godforsaken town far, far behind...

I broke out of the trance, and she was still talking. Her voice grated my shot nerves. She wanted to have 'make-up sex,' like 'real' couples do. A wave of nausea hit my stomach. The last time we had had sex, it was after she'd had another man over for dinner. I'd seen the receipts in the trash, the leftovers, the new condoms in her purse. She'd seduced me to cover her tracks, just in case... Afterward, I'd felt violated, like I was a stranger in my own body. I'd made up some excuse to go outside so I could throw up. I hadn't made that mistake again.

I turned to her, accepted her apology, and then returned to the couch. The corners of my eyes had an excess of moisture... but no. I couldn't show any more weakness. I pushed it all away, reached over, and dragged the mutts into their preferred positions. Then I opened up the laptop and started to research the divorce process. It was time.

It took me most of the night to fill out the forms. The offer was generous, 50% of all my assets and shared custody of the dogs. An online attorney had done the legal legwork.

When she emerged from the bedroom the next morning, there was a stack of paperwork on the table for her to sign. Her initial curiosity was quickly replaced with contempt.

"So that's it?" she asked. One of her eyebrows was raised comically high. Until then I hadn't noticed that she was plucking them. I started to reply, and she cut me off.

"You chose this," she said.

The melodramatic air of finality hung in the air. It was starkly juxtaposed by the entrance of one of the dogs. His tail was wagging furiously as he roared in and buried his face in my lap. I looked down at both of them, gave them a tight squeeze, then watched as Delilah slung a massive bag over her shoulder and left, slamming the door behind her. I held my breath until the sounds of my car tearing off across the parking lot faded.

This is going to hurt.

28

KEY WEST

The flight was the bumpiest I had ever experienced. The plane rocked and rattled, eliciting the occasional scream from one of the other passengers. Midflight, an overhead compartment flew open and spilled bags onto the heads of an entire row. Even the flight attendants were rattled. When the plane landed, everyone clapped and laughed... I could hear it through the pair of headphones one of Delilah's boyfriends had left in my truck. The noise-canceling was amazing, aside from that.

The weather in Paradise was shit, but I wasn't there on vacation. I beelined to an indoor bar I knew and put those bartenders to work. By noon, the water was starting to slough off the streets. The puddles rapidly drained into the sand beneath, almost as fast as the margaritas they were putting in front of me.

"You're not driving, eh?" the bartender asked, flashing a grin.

"I'm here to bury my father," I said in a flat monotone. Then I drained the rest of my glass and set into the next. He didn't ask any more questions after that.

A few hours later, the clouds cleared. It was time. My phone emitted a warning klaxon. A message from Delilah. That hadn't happened in a while. She was thoroughly enjoying our separation. She had the house, car, dog, and the business. I had a backpack, laptop, and a box of ashes that was currently sitting next to an empty piña colada on a dirty bar top. I ordered three beers and stuffed them into my backpack.

The ashes had sat in my brother's closet for years. I tried for years to get him to talk about it, but he still blamed me for... all of it. He'd clung to the bag of carcinogens and burnt cancer with a fervent intensity. Finally, my mother had interceded and mailed them across the country. They had arrived in a cookie tin. Within was a plastic bag that smelled of burnt barbecue and ash. I'd bought a fancy box to put them in. Everyone deserves that much.

The fancy box had sat on the corner of my desk for months, watching my marriage dissolve. Unwittingly, and decidedly not deliberately, my father was forced to see my life. I talked to him often. As usual, he never responded.

His partner had kept the other half of the ashes. She'd poured them out at sea years before. Which meant that the job was only half-finished. And every man, regardless of his sins, deserves to be fully buried. One cannot progress into whatever comes next with one foot caught in the doorway, and I highly doubted he would want to live through eternity as a paperweight, even if the box was really nice.

So there we were, at the entryway to the Caribbean, the seat of every Jimmy Buffett song and marimba band one could be bothered to listen to. I did my best to try and enjoy it. It certainly wasn't my first time there. I had some great memories on these streets, but it's hard to fully enjoy a place when your heart is torn in half and your mind is constantly being yanked into the deepest and blackest depths. There was only one way out and I knew it.

Through.

I stumbled out of the bar, hit the slick pavement, and deftly slid across the sidewalk. The box of ashes was tucked under my arm like a football. A bikini-clad woman laughed and held up a drink in toast. I blew her a kiss and asked her to marry me. The joke was lost on her. As I walked away, she mentioned that I was already wearing a wedding ring. But she couldn't possibly understand. Delilah certainly wasn't wearing hers.

It didn't take long to get to the pier. There were so many of them, I couldn't tell which one was the right one. He had told me a story... But that was a long time ago. It didn't matter. Any of them would do.

I found an open bench that wasn't too covered in bird shit and plopped down. A sign ahead promised strict penalties for alcohol use. Oh well. Sometimes you've just got to pay the damn fine.

I set the box on the bench beside me and cracked two beers. I paired two sets of headphones to my phone, placed one of them where I would imagine his ears to be, and took a long swig. I played Jimmy Buffett, Bob Marley, and Jerry Jeff Walker. I also played him some new stuff that I thought he'd like. We sat there and talked for a long time, tourists passing all around, seagulls calling and pelicans floating on the breeze.

The time came suddenly. I had finished my beers and started on his. The music had long ceased to play. I didn't know how long I had been silent. The sun had taken its inexorable slant down the horizon, now casting deep red and orange brush strokes across the heavily pressing cloud cover. Something held back. Held on. I paused. Minutes stretched and stacked on top of one another. I clutched the box in my arm. People gave me a wide berth.

"What the hell do I do about *this*?" I whispered.

As usual, he said nothing. Birds squawked and darted across the waves. Somewhere in the distance, a horn sonorously called out across the island.

In one swift motion, I pulled the lid off of the box, opened the plastic bag within, and poured the remains into the warm, surging water beneath the pier. The ashes floated, a greasy stain pulsing and radiating before the individual grains began to slowly sink. Deeper. Ever deeper. The box sat on the concrete ledge, underneath the rusted green bars.

"Not so bad, Dad," I said, my voice cracking.

The sides of my face were wet, somehow. I watched the stain smear into nothingness, then turned, slid sunglasses over my eyes, and walked back to the beach.

I didn't have much time. My bus left within the hour.

29

DOA

The day was a smoldering fire smothered by the weight of a wet blanket. The world smelled like a fart let loose beneath the sheets. My life was catastrophically fucked. Everything was done, kaput, forever burned. I sat in my '95 Ranger, a limping, battered truck that was supposed to be a project. I was making my way through my second pack of cigarettes. The smoke curled along the coffee-spattered cloth seats and the sun-stained dashboard.

Hours before, I had been in the sheriff's office. The call had come in while I was installing new locks on the front door. My life had fallen apart right there in front of me.

***

"We called you in here to inform you that she has filed a protective order—"

"A... A wha— Against me?!"

"Yes, sir. You'll have to vacate your home immediately. Stay away from her... and her friends, evidently. And we'll have to confiscate your guns."

"My house? Guns? But she threatened to shoot me last week! She—"

"Sir."

"You guys were there yesterday! I didn't do anything!"

"Sir."

"She's mentally unstable! And a pathological liar!"

"That doesn't matter, sir."

"Doesn't matter??? What the fuck? So she can cheat on me in my own bed, hit me, scream at me, and now she gets to take everything I own, with no proof—"

"Evidently she had some videos to show the judge."

"Videos? Of what? Can I see these?"

"No, sir."

...

...

"This was her plan all along."

"It... appears that way. Sir."

***

The full weight crushed me into the seat so hard that I thought my ribcage would snap at any moment. I was in shock. My breath came ragged, each one brusquely torn from the bottom of my chest by the small part of me that actually wanted to live. Plumes of smoke rose and coalesced against the narrow roof above.

I had gone to the park, my dogs' favorite place. It was all I could think to do. I couldn't go home. I would most likely never see their scruffy faces ever again. The road had swerved and wobbled in my vision so much that I had barely made it. My face itched, canyons of salt forming along well-traveled routes. Waves of numbness coated my body and brain. Something ancient and primitive was trying to protect me. From myself or from the outside world was anyone's guess.

I hated her. I loved her. I hated... No. I refused. This had been her plan all along. She had masterfully maneuvered me. I was completely defeated. I had been hoodwinked, humiliated, and cast aside. But there was one thing I could still control. I refused to hate. Because that would mean that I was just like her.

As I pulled off the road, I noticed the car next to me like you would notice a slightly stunted tree in a forest. It was just an obstacle, easily disregarded. Cars, bikes, and stroller-pushers passed down the dirt track. None of them meant anything. I couldn't remember how to do basic things. My hands shook violently. I was falling, fast and furious, the air rushing past my ears with a shrill whistle.

The dust was still settling around the truck when my gut twisted violently. Something churned, wrenching my head, pulling me out of shock. Something was wrong, even more wrong than what was happening in my life. I pulled myself from the driver's seat, stood on quaking legs, and started to look around—

Twenty feet away, a woman was laid out on the grass. She hadn't been there when I pulled in. I gaped for a long second. Then a bubble began to slowly emerge from her mouth... it popped. My phone appeared at my ear. Something else had dialed the number. A familiar voice came through. 911.

I described the situation and received my instructions. Open the airway. Head against the chest. Compression. Compression. Rescue breaths. Good God, the smell. Good God, the *taste*. Head against the chest. Compressions—

A last spasm wracked the woman's body. Her chest seized, all of the muscles and sinew pulling tight, almost to snapping... I watched the life leave her body, feeling the aftershocks ripple across her nerves. The blood began to slow... and with a heavy sigh, she was gone.

You're such a piece of shit.

Something snapped in the deepest, most heavily sedated folds of my brain. I had been thrown from the mountain, bouncing, folding, and breaking on the way down. I had paused, my momentum slowed, on a narrow rock outcropping. This was the rock that had followed closely behind, kicking me back into free fall.

I kneeled, my kneecaps damp on the wet grass, watching a bubble rise from her face, blue and pale in the bright morning light. Her body was twisted, hands contorted into grotesque formations. Her face was a rictus of pain, but her eyes... they were a light blue, like the morning sky after a long winter's night. They were at peace. At ease. I reached forward and gently pulled the skin over them. My hand stayed on her face, already cooling rapidly.

The paramedics arrived shortly after. A giant man gently led me away. He was gruff and stern until he saw my face. Then he softened, running a hand across my shoulders. He said nothing after that, simply standing, saying nothing as I lit my third cigarette with the end of the second.

When the sheriff showed up, she stared at me. It was the same one that I had seen minutes before, guilty before proven innocent. Her disbelief was plain. You could watch the inner-machinations clunking and breaking down across the broad expanse of her face. The sense of humor of whatever deity was running that show was grim indeed.

A crowd had appeared, all staring as the corpse was covered with a blanket, then hauled into the back of the ambulance. I hadn't moved. There was nowhere to go. I could feel the dark tendrils of instinct and survival digging their way to the forefront. My vision narrowed to a thin tube, the totality of existence simplified to the sparsest thread. Everything was gone. These were the last grains of sand from a castle that had been abandoned to the tide. And yet…

A shock of sunlight flashed through the pines above. It could be worse. Much, much worse. I had been shattered to shards before. I was an expert at making something from nothing. This would be my greatest test, my *pièce de résistance*, a swan song of survival that would echo triumphantly through the remainder of my life. I just had to survive until it was completed. I knew then, with the certainty of an intelligence far above what I could conjure, that if I didn't get to work, I would end up just like this.

Eventually, the crowd dispersed. The last to leave was the sheriff. She stared at me for another second, still appraising, then nodded. Her squad car went slowly at first, then the lights flashed on and she roared off into the abyss. The sun was starting to go down when I ran out of cigarettes.

***

I leaned back and felt the oppressive weight press me back into the leather seats. I had the seat warmer on, despite the heat and humidity pulsing in waves from the opened window. My body was always cold. Every few hours or so, a stinging pain would come from another finger gone numb. I would shake them gently, trying not to disturb the puppy asleep on my lap. We drove endlessly, the road stretching out ahead, forever calling a siren's song, luring me out into the depths…

She'd gotten the condo. The one I had bought for us. The first place I had ever felt safe and at home. Despite the simmering rage, I had to hand it to her. She was like the evil opera singer, the fervent storm of her contralto echoing through each and every lie... She'd even taken time to break down crying in the hallway. It was a masterful performance. I was the only one who wasn't fooled.

I looked down at the dog asleep on my lap. She had engineered a "reconciliation," then insisted that we get him. I now knew why that was. Our other dog was registered as my service animal. She hadn't wanted to give him up. And she knew that I wouldn't abandon a puppy. I ruffled the little guy's ears, and he dug further into my lap.

"You're good enough," I said to him.

The road stretched out ahead. I thought of the woman, dying alone on the side of the road. My dreams were haunted by images of my home and bubbles slowly popping... These were my warnings. I could have lived an entire life asleep, or taken the easy way out. I knew this was a reckoning, a forced realignment. I had been pushed off course by a storm and forced to navigate uncharted waters. But still...

I couldn't see the point of it all. I also couldn't see past my fingertips. I drove completely on autopilot, my body doing what it had been trained to do. I was a fragile reed adrift in the middle of a raging river. There was no telling how far I would go on any given day, or where I would end up for the night. Nothing mattered. All I could do was keep a cigarette in one hand and my puppy's smooth fur underneath the other.

I had been conned, robbed, belittled, cheated, and demeaned. I had let myself fall into... whatever this was. There was nothing to turn to. The only firm handhold was on the steering wheel. My only friends were the snoring ball in my lap and the smoothly undulating turns ahead. I vowed right then to never let another human being put me in a situation like this. They could tear my self-respect from my cold, dead hands.

I could no longer be the person that I had been. I was gutted and shattered, a massacre of formerly coherent pieces. But I had been here before. I knew exactly how to endure. The darkness was all-encompassing, the world collected in a ragged band of enemies, all bent on self-aggrandizement. But these monsters had no idea who they were fucking with.

I had built entire lives around women and other people, tethering my sense of purpose and self-worth to illusory, ever-changing mindsets. My life had been defined by one singular purpose: finding people to love me. And that pursuit had left me with nothing. This was as low as I could go.

The silver lining was obvious. This pile of wreckage cleared the way for something new to be built, something stronger, quieter, and far more reserved. I could find new pieces and assemble them any way I wanted. Everything had to change. I had to become the best version of myself, cast in a mold of my own choosing.

I knew then, that I was finally done falling.

I leaned into the curves and felt the warm breath on my leg. The road drove itself. One question remained.

Who do I want to be now?

30

Epilogue

I'd caught her red-handed.

Over the past year, I had watched her desperately try to get rises out of me. The assault was continuous, a never-ending flow of dog-whistles, gaslighting, and ad hominem attacks. Every moment spent with her felt wasted. My duty had ended. Only inertia kept me within her orbit.

I had the email laid out on the table. It was a damning exposé of her behavior that completely contradicted everything she had been saying to me for the past weeks. Everything out of her mouth had been a blatant lie. And like peeling back one layer of an onion, the second I saw the exposed truth, more layers began to appear. Within minutes, I had grasped the entire situation, stretching back years. I saw, with brutal clarity, how thoroughly I had been used and deceived. And I was relieved.

I would later go through the machinations. Grief, despair, rage, hatred... all would have their turn. There are still nights when I wake up with balled fists, a younger version of myself standing up at the foot of the bed... But in that moment, I felt the soothing balm of release. The crushing weight of an entire ancestral line fell from my shoulders in one breath. I no longer had any reason to stay.

I stared at the screen as she entered the room. When I looked up, she had seen it as well. She seemed much older then, as if the past month had worn on her as fiercely as me. But I knew it was just the alcohol. It was 2 p.m. She thought I didn't know about the pile of bottles beneath the couch, or the real reason for her 'stomach troubles.' I knew she was headed for a nap. It usually took an hour or two for her to sober up enough to get ready to go out for dinner.

"I saw the email," I said. I could hear the coldness in my voice. I had no more energy left to waste. "Do you want to talk about it, or should I just leave?"

That's all it took. Whatever small threads she had been holding onto were now clearly torn. I watched impassively as she tried every trick, threw every barb, desperately hurling venom in a last-ditch attempt to hurt me. None of it worked.

I thought of my father then. I remembered his deeply pleading eyes, the gentleness of his final movements, the repentance in his face. He had been easy to forgive because he had actually been willing to admit that he was wrong. This woman never would. Her ego and pride were too massive. She would never apologize, never admit her faults, never attempt to be human. She was a waste of my time.

I looked up from the laptop, into her eyes, and felt nothing.

The desperation intensified, then changed, and behind the alcohol and ego, something else emerged: Hate. Pure, unadulterated hate. Her eyes shone with a kaleidoscope of antipathies and hostilities. For some reason, however, this was amusing. A sense of finality came over the scene. She couldn't hurt me anymore.

I was free.

"You wanted a daughter so bad, you lost a son," I said, chuckling. It was amusing. God help me, I had been waiting for this. For an excuse, to unchain me from the bindings of being a 'good son.' I looked up to the ceiling, thinking there should be something else to say... Oh, yeah.

"Don't contact me."

She was ranting again as I turned and left the room, but I couldn't hear. I slung my bag over my shoulder and walked out the back door. The wooden staircase that I had painted and repaired squeaked lightly underneath my boots. The door handle was loose again, and the gate out to the street was riding high... Oh, well. Someone else's problem now.

A half-block away, my phone chimed. I deleted the message without looking and blocked the number. I knew I would never be back. There was no point pretending otherwise.

Ahead of me was a thick, well-manicured rose bush in full bloom. It was the first place I stopped when I came back in off the road. It was the scent of 'home.' I grabbed a two-fisted heap of the dark red roses and, ignoring the thorns pressing into my palms, deeply inhaled. The smell dominated, pushing deeply into my sinuses. It was a subtle, silent exclamation point; a firm yet fleeting kiss on the cheek. It was goodbye.

And it smelled *great*.

31

Acknowledgments

To, in absolutely no order: Stefan Prodanovic (my amazing cover artist), Arya, Mr. Gallatti, Shane, The Sanctuary, my neighbor down the street who let me steal her flowers for dates, Mason, the guy on the corner who yelled at everyone but me, Tickets (you tried), Brian, the cab driver in Marrakech, Sunshine, Mike, the shuttle driver at Crater Lake in 2017, Mahmoud, Mike & Tom, the bartenders at the Triple Nickel, Benji, D, Pete Bernhard, Jenn, the owners of the Londonderry Inn, ChatGPT, Anton, Kasandra, Andy, the cooks from Useppa Island, Rowdy, whoever left 'Happy Birthday' on my door at Ranchos de los Caballeros, Eve, Chef Raquel, the fine folks of Hyampom, Camp Namanu, Chris, AJ, Polly, Cindy, the guy who hooked me up with a free year of internet in college, Marc, Tom, the hostel in Denver that paid for my bed and my pawn-shopped camera, Missy, Bailey, Ken, Billy, everyone who ever held a door open for me, Yu Ping, Mr. Bojangles, Oregon Music News, Appsketiers, Timm, Namu, The Chakra House, the guy in the Camaro, Dan The Man, that one bouncer in Portland who saved my life, everyone who ever let me ride in the back of their pickup, Monk, the Italian FBI of Formia, Georgie, that guy in the medina who zipped up my backpack, Tim, everyone who bought my first book, Abbie, the Chinese place in Hendersonville, Bon Paul & Sharky's Hostel, Tickled Pink (I still remember that ice cold six pack), Jeffy, Erik, that woman in Denver who handed me a $100 bill, Joni, Matt Link (thanks for treating me like a human being),

Dr. Hagopian, Allie, The Stag, Rosie, Mr. Lehman, the administrative team at Braxton Place, The Silver Dollar, Jeremy, Lewis, Cutty, Chally, the beautiful fuckers at - , Irie G, the guy in Tulum who handed me a face mask and a pair of shades when I couldn't keep it in anymore, the Uber driver who brought back my phone all that way, everyone who has ever worked in a SNAP office, Sheri, the man who taught me yoga, Mr. Halpern, Aunt Claude, Shane's Brother, all the beta readers I've ever had, Adelle, Kyle, and KC, Coffee Time, and everyone who ever hurt me on purpose.

And most importantly, to Rambo — you never wavered. 'Til the end, my friend.

If I forgot anyone or anything, I'll get you on the next go around.

Follow the rest of the story at:

scsanborn.com

www.ingramcontent.com/pod-product-compliance
Lightning Source LLC
LaVergne TN
LVHW091249080426
835510LV00007B/186